Contents

Good Design for DTP Users

A J Marlow

NCC Blackwell

MANCHESTER • OXFORD

British Library Cataloguing in Publication Data

Marlow, A. J.
Good design for DTP users
1. Desktop publishing

I. Title
070.50285416

ISBN 0-85012-793-9

Published for NCC Publications by NCC Blackwell Limited.

Editorial Office: The National Computing Centre Limited, Oxford Road, Manchester M1 7ED, England.

NCC Blackwell Limited, 108 Cowley Road, Oxford OX4 1JF, England.

Typeset in 11pt Dutch using Aldus PageMaker version 3.0 and a Hewlett Packard LaserJet series II; and printed by Hobbs the Printers of Southampton.

ISBN 0-85012-793-9

Acknowledgements

For discussion on specific points I am grateful to a number of friends, correspondents and colleagues. I am also grateful to the following organisations: Aldus Corporation, Hewlett Packard Company and Compugraphic Corporation. Thanks are also due to the staff of NCC Blackwell for all their efforts.

This book owes much, especially in the final stages of production, to the dedicated and competent efforts of Brenda Durndell.

Acknowledgements are due to the following for some of the illustration material: Linotype and Machinery Ltd; Le Départment de l'Instruction Publique, Geneva; Pro Helvetia, Zurich; and the Swiss Federal Statistical Office, Berne, for permission to use the information shown in the table examples.

Preface

The reason for understanding typographical concepts, in respect of your desktop publishing system, is so that you are better equipped to improve the design of the material that you produce, to make it as easy as possible for readers to understand the message, and for you to convey the kind of image and visual effect that will both attract and keep the attention of the reader.

This book aims to acquaint the untrained designer with some of the principles of typography and design with respect to desktop publishing systems, without being specific to any particular system. Today, many of the higher quality desktop publishing software packages provide helpful advice about layout and design, and even standard formats on which you can base your own publications. Some of the less well-known and cheaper packages do not. Even those that provide design assistance in the form of templates and style sheets do not explain *why* particular designs are the way they are, what makes a good layout, or what elements of design have been applied to their examples.

By finding out about the basic principles of typography, and thereby appreciating what makes a design good or bad, you can begin to explore beyond the examples that your software documentation provides. To be able to do this requires experience and knowledge. With this book, the quest for that knowledge begins.

It is all too easy to be constrained by the designs suggested for particular types of document, by working through a book of layouts or by using a template for a particular job. If you learn the fundamentals for yourself, you will be better equipped to experiment with confidence.

You should understand that the typesetting features covered in this book may not be available on all desktop publishing systems. For example, some of the cheaper software packages do not provide a facility for the fine adjustment of spacing between words and letters. The type of equipment that you have may determine what kind of effects are possible with your system. The features of PostScript laser printers may be greater than PCL printers in terms of the choice of typeface, the control over the size and position of characters, and the provision of certain effects, such as rotated and reversed out (white out of black) text, etc.

Reading about features that your system does not have may help you to assess whether you think they might be useful to you and, therefore, whether you might consider upgrading your software to a package that offers a more comprehensive range of facilities. However, this rather depends upon the applications for which you use your desktop publishing system. The more variety required from the output, the more control over the design elements you will want. You will need to refer to your desktop publishing software documentation to find out how to implement some of the features described, since the different software packages achieve results in a variety of ways. Terminology can also vary slightly, though most systems use standard publishing terms such as 'point size' for the size of a typeface, 'justification' for alignment of text to margins, and so on.

While many of the topics in such a book are subjective (for example, you may disagree with some concepts on the effects of design choices on the readability of a document), if you have been encouraged to think about design more than you may have previously done, then this book will have achieved its objectives.

A J Marlow MSc
Titchmarsh, 1990

1 Introduction

DTP USERS

As a user of desktop publishing, (DTP), you are likely to fall into one of three categories of user:

— those who are 'professionals' (typesetters, designers, printers, etc) and are perhaps using this relatively new technology in place of more traditional facilities for type and design;

— those who are 'semi-skilled' with certain keyboard and document layout skills previously acquired using typewriters and word processors, and are looking to upgrade the quality of output and extend the capabilities of the type of work you produce;

— and, finally, those who are 'unskilled' and are using desktop publishing to satisfy a number of artwork and layout requirements hitherto produced for you by professionals and now within your jurisdiction; perhaps with a view to saving costs and enhancing the appearance of your publications.

These categories are generalisations of what is, in reality, a much more complex and detailed sub-set of uses for desktop publishing. Yet for those people with no formal design skills (ie those who do not fall into the 'professionals' category), the degree to which the use of your desktop publishing system is realised will depend upon you acquiring, by tuition and experience, as many of the skills of good design as you can. It is for you that this book is primarily intended.

For those of you working in busy offices and commercial organisations, spending sufficient time in learning and training is often a difficult thing to achieve. So often, little time is set aside for learning new skills, while most time is concentrated on what *has* to be done. Training courses are available, which cover the principles of good design, and there are those which concentrate on particular desktop publishing packages. If possible, try and attend these courses, since they take you away from your normal working environment and give you the chance to get to know a great deal about design skills with direct relevance to the type of system you are using.

EMPHASIS OF THE BOOK

This book is intended as an introduction to some of the basic principles of typesetting and design, with particular emphasis given to the use of desktop publishing systems. There are many other books on design, some of which deal with the design of a specific type of publication (such as book design), while others cover specific desktop publishing software systems which, apart from giving some hints towards design, often repeat much of the information already covered in the instruction manuals. In contrast to these publications, this book is a general introduction to the various aspects and terminology of design. Use the book as a means of learning the fundamentals, then build on the topics using experience and by seeking further tuition.

Learning the Basics

Desktop publishing has come in for some severe criticism from the professional and traditional designers. It is thought that the technology for specialist design, typography and graphics, being so readily available on standard microcomputers, is in the hands of a large number of people who don't know what to do with it. Unskilled designers are now designing their own publications, forms and business stationery. Typists and secretaries are being given the tools to produce artwork for which they have not even a basic training. The result of this situation, 'they' say, is that there is a glut of badly designed material being published by a lot of people who are simply playing with the tools of a professional and highly skilled trade. An analogous situation could be seen in providing a layperson with the tools and materials to build a house. The question is, even given the plans, can the layperson successfully build a house, simply by having the right tools, or is it fair to say that to build a good wall, you need bricklaying skills? If you are honest, the answer should be 'no'. So, are all these criticisms fair? Well, yes. If you are going to use desktop publishing properly, you have a responsibility to maintain a certain standard of output quality and a duty to improve your skills in this area, if you wish to escape the criticism.

But this does not mean that you have to adhere to a set of rules about design which guarantee success! Actually, a great deal of opinion about design is largely personal. Any two books about the best way to typeset tabular work will probably give two conflicting opinions. Much more important is that you understand the *fundamental* aspects of good design. Knowing what makes a design good or bad is not simply a matter of solving an equation — if design type 'A' does not look like 'X', then it is bad. In many respects, design is a highly subjective matter, and what pleases the eye of one person is not guaranteed to please another. Experience will play an important part of your learning, but you will need to train your eye so you know why one design looks better than another, even if it is only in your opinion, and not because a design book says so.

There are 'rules' for good typesetting, but it is probably more accurate to say that they are tried and tested solutions for improving the appearance of text in certain conditions and for certain types of publication. There are usually several solutions to a single design problem, many of which may all be suitable. But there are certainly things which you should *not* do if you are to avoid defeating the object of any publication, which is that it should convey its message clearly to the intended reader. What makes good typography is often a result of our prejudices, which are themselves based on what is familiar to us. In the English-speaking world, the use of certain typefaces in particular circumstances, the layout used in newspapers and books, on signs and notices, in magazines and brochures, all follow familiar patterns. When we deviate greatly from these norms, the result often subconsciously unsettles the reader. 'Rules are made to be broken', goes the saying, which is all very well, provided we are prepared for the consequences.

Appropriate Typography

Most books are typeset in what is called a 'book face'. This is a typeface which is easy to read in long passages, and you will learn more about this in Chapters 3 and 4. If a book were to be set in a fancy and decorative typestyle it may look pleasant at a glance, but if it makes the reading difficult and slow, it will hardly be appropriate for the purpose, and will not be acceptable for the mass paperback, non-fiction market. Being *appropriate* is what good design is all about, and this is more important to remember than a whole set of rules.

The more you learn about design, the more knowledge and relevant information you will have to bring to bear on your next design and publication task. I have seen many examples of output from unskilled people using desktop publishing which are mostly quite acceptable. Professional designers might call them bad designs, but this can often be an overreaction, and an emotional response in defence of their skills and knowledge. In truth, what a professional might call bad is only relative; the average layperson receiving the material will probably be none the wiser and completely unaware of the so-called pitfalls and design errors made by the desktop publishing system operator who produced the publication.

However, it is probably true to say that many designs from unskilled hands can be improved, and the improvement may not be apparent until alternative design possibilities are examined side by side. Attaining skills in design means acquiring sufficient experience and understanding to be able to arrive at an optimum design in fewer steps than the novice. The finer points of typography are seemingly irrelevant to many of the tasks for which desktop publishing is employed. For example, some research into typography has found a connection with the legibility of a particular design and the choice of typeface. The legibility of a typeface is said to be influenced by factors affecting the reader, such as his or her mood at the time (for example, whether one is angry or not), the alertness, tiredness, age or sex of the reader, and so on. While these may be accurate findings under research conditions, one can hardly expect the average desktop publishing operator to even give a second's thought to their importance before deciding on the most appropriate design for a company press release or product newsletter. Even after considering fine adjustments to character and word spacing, which may result in subtle changes to the appearance of the text, these will probably escape the notice of the reader altogether. This is perhaps fortunate, since many of these subtleties are beyond the capabilities of a standard desktop publishing system in any case.

Appropriate Design

This does highlight one basic principle which is worth remembering, whatever the type of publication job you are undertaking. The conveyance of the message within a publications is, with few exceptions, more important than the manner in which it is conveyed. In other words, the reader's attention should not be diverted from the message by the style of type or the overall design. If a design detracts from the message, the publication is more than likely failing to fulfill its original purpose. A design must not lead to ambiguities in the content of the publication. Spacing, typestyle and layout, use of illustrations and other factors can all affect the ability of a publication to effectively communicate its message, and you must always keep this point in mind — it is of far more importance than the æsthetic qualities of a publication. The golden rule for unskilled designers is *keep it simple, keep it clear*.

Improving Skills

In time, familiarity with different design effects will enable you to add more flair to your publications. One of the most widely seen errors in the output from desktop publishing systems by unskilled users is the over use of design facilities: too many typestyles are used, too many sizes of characters, too many graphics, rules and icons. The suitability of a design is discussed in more detail in Chapter 15. Other chapters cover various related topics concerning design, though rarely do any individual topics have meaning on their own. They have been separated in this book so that you may easily refer to them at a later date to refresh your memory, and they do not follow a particular order of importance.

Related Topics

The last two chapters of the book cover areas outside the direct use of desktop publishing systems, but which are indirectly associated with the complete design process. These are the processes of print production (covered in Chapter 16) and various means of print finishing (covered in Chapter 17). They introduce the importance of considering a publication as a whole. Even if the operator of the desktop publishing system may be responsible for only the design of a job and not the printing, he or she must consider other factors, such as how the publication is to be presented, bound, or despatched. These factors may, for example, affect the width of margins used, paper size, layout, typesize, and so on. For those individuals who may have an overall responsibility for publications within an organisation, it is part of their duty to see that the operator of the desktop publishing system is given sufficient information to enable correct design judgements to be made.

THE TECHNOLOGY

As electronic publishing technology advances, the distinction between standard word processing and desktop publishing becomes diminished. Many so-called word processing packages combine many features of typesetting, together with advanced facilities for the handling and manipulation of graphics images. No longer is there the need for glue and scissors to enable you to include graphs and drawings into reports and brochures; this is now provided for with electronic cut and paste facilities. With such an abundance of facilities at the fingertips of those using word processors of this kind, many operators have more functions available than they know how to handle. So many features are either ignored or misused. In an effort to make the most of these software and hardware capabilities, this book provides a first step towards improving the understanding of design and layout principles which these facilities are provided for.

The Design Process

It has been normal for many professional designers to rough out their layouts and design on layout paper with the aid of a spacing grid, using pencils and rulers and producing what are known as 'design roughs'. For them, desktop publishing enables these mock-up designs to be produced quickly, using the same equipment that may be used for the production of the final artwork. It also means that designers working for clients and printers can produce far more accurate and completed examples for approval, which is beneficial to both parties.

For the less skilled, the use of desktop publishing for practising layout ideas is easier than working on paper, for it requires fewer artistic skills. Planning designs on paper requires considerable experience and a trained ability with a pen and pencil. Today, these tools are increasingly being replaced with a mouse and screen so that areas of text and images can be moved, sized and repositioned until a satisfactory design emerges, with not a single sheet of paper being used until the printed version is required.

The entire design process can be one of editing a basic set of objects (be they blocks of text or graphics) until the components fit together in a meaningful way, and with an appearance which is both effective and pleasing to the eye. Using the same typefaces at the rough planning stages that may be used on the finished job is important when practising with designs, since the way text conveys a message changes subtly from one typeface to another. By using the typefaces that are available on the desktop publishing system, one can get an immediate impression of how effective a particular publication will be before being committed to producing the final copies or artwork for reproduction.

Traditionally, the publishing process was broken down into three distinct areas of production:

a) the creation of copy (the text);
b) manipulation (positioning of the design elements); and
c) the typesetting.

Today, desktop publishing systems handle all three processes in the one domain. The operator can not only prepare the copy and store it on disk for future retrieval and editing, but, using the same text files, is able to prepare a layout using graphics tools and 'paste' the text into the format, adding the appropriate style and typeface information at the same time. This contrasts with a traditional form of preparation where the copy would have been marked-up with instructions for the typesetter operator about the indentation, style, spacing and typeface requirements. To mark-up copy in this way required sufficient experience and knowledge of typesetting to allow the marker to envisage or imagine how the finished work would appear after typesetting.

Using the Technology in Design

Desktop publishing systems often work by using style names or paragraph 'tags' attached to a block of text; these carry all the design attributes of the text within the chosen block. With these the operator can simply change one or more aspects of the style information for that change to be reflected immediately throughout the entire publication, affecting each block of text carrying the appropriate style name.

These new ways of working are relevant to the process of learning design and layout because they affect the way in which one can learn about good design. By using these characteristics of desktop publishing, the operator can learn about the effect of many of the features described in this book by trying out various settings and ideas on a practice document, and watching the process of typography in operation on the screen before them. Compared with the previous generation of typographers and designers, the modern desktop publishing system user has got it made!

GENERAL

In Chapter 2, there is a brief introduction to the history of typography. It is not essential reading, and indeed, the progress of typesetting has advanced so much in the last few years that one does not have to go back far to review the traditional methods of typesetting and printing. The purpose of the chapter is for those who wish to have a historical background to the subject for the sake of satisfying their own personal interest, but also to help clarify some of the origins of the terminology which survives in desktop publishing, even though the methods employed are now far removed from their origins.

Chapter 3 introduces the nature of type; explaining the two main classes of typeface and providing a background on the variety of typefaces which exist. You will learn some of the terminology used to describe type and the way it looks. This is followed by more information about specific typefaces and styles, why they are used and how you can use them to best effect. In addition to the choice of typeface and style, the choice of size of the type, and its spacing (both interlinear — line spacing — and between words and characters), has a strong influence on the overall appearance, and this is covered in later chapters. The remaining chapters of the book cover particular areas of design and layout, with information on special topics such as tables, headings, illustration captions and title pages.

You are not obliged to follow the book through in sequence. Any topic can be read in isolation, but you may find that, should you choose to read a chapter in isolation, assumptions are made about knowledge of topics introduced in any earlier chapters. Some of the information provided is useful for reference purposes, such as spacing tables, paper size details and so on. For this reason, subjects are organised under headings which should help you to refer back to particular information, although there is undoubtedly some overlap from one topic to another throughout the book.

It is worth re-stating that no specific make of desktop publishing system is particularly considered when mentioning the facilities within this book, and some suggestions about layout and design may not be possible with some of the more basic and less expensive software packages. The book aims to cover principles irrespective of the system used to produce the artwork, so that the information contained in it is less likely to become outdated as technology moves ahead. Neither is output quality mentioned, so it does not matter whether you use a laser printer, dot matrix printer or digital phototypesetter for your output device, when you look at the details in the remainder of this book.

2 Typography – a Brief History

EARLY EFFORTS

From the earliest form of writing, one can trace the history of typography. Even the illuminated manuscripts of the Magna Carta offer an example of some of the most decorative typography in history. Perhaps surprisingly, some of the earliest writings provide the finest examples of penmanship with considerable quality of letter form and layout. The written works not only recorded history but the day-to-day transactions and communications of their time. The chronicles were naturally quite laborious efforts, and the reproduction of these documents required the employment of a great number of resources, otherwise they took a very long time to achieve. Those persons in religious establishments, who had the benefit of learning how to read and write were certainly in the minority of the population, hence, in the Middle Ages, much of the copying of books and manuscripts was carried out by monks. The monks copied ancient manuscripts, written in Latin or Greek, on calfskin or sheepskin called 'vellum'. These 'scribes' who had, not only the ability, but the time to devote to the task, kept much of the literature of the past for future generations. The hand-written manuscripts are art treasures in their own right – beautiful examples of typography, often with large embellished capital letters, and borders decorated with designs of flowers, vines, birds and other pictures in green, gold, blue and red (an example is shown in Figure 2.1).

While all this was going on in medieval Europe, the Chinese had been using porcelain character blocks to reproduce images for centuries. They were created by moulding or carving out a reversal of the image or character to be printed. The raised images were then inked and paper was then pressed onto the surface to give a faithful reproduction each time (at least until the blocks became worn or damaged). This form of reproduction was taking place as early as the 7th or 8th century AD and can be considered to be the earliest form of producing type mechanically. Moveable type or blocks, each carved with an individual character, were introduced later on in China, around the 11th century AD. This method of reproduction enabled the characters to be arranged for printing one job, then taken apart and rearranged for the next job. The developments in China did not make significant progress, possibly due to the thousands of characters in their alphabet which would have made the process extremely cumbersome to handle.

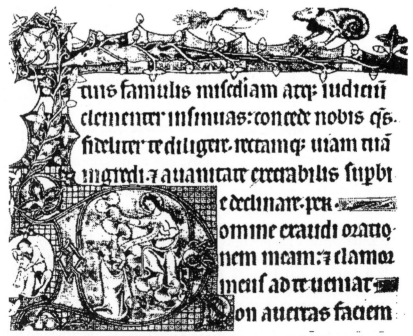

Figure 2.1   Example of Illuminated Manuscript

At the beginning of the 14th century the Koreans started using interchangeable copper blocks, and even wooden blocks were being used in Europe for printing images (other than the type) or perhaps single capital letters in manuscripts. For the Europeans, the Black Death put an end to many of the literate members of the community and so the scribes, whose job it was to reproduce the books and documents of the time, were not only becoming scarce, but consequently an expensive commodity. However, at that time, the availability of paper was not a problem, as newly established paper mills were producing vast quantities of material at very low costs, compared to parchment.

Further Developments

The scene was set for a new development to take advantage of the situation and, in the 15th century, a goldsmith called Johann Gansfleisch, from Mainz, in Germany (better known by his adopted mother's surname of Gutenberg) pioneered the development of moveable type, made from cast metal characters (putting his skills in working with soft metals to good use). The type had to be uniform in size, and relatively hard wearing. Accurate casting was necessary so that the characters would align evenly and fit tightly together, so that an even line of print would result. Each letter was cast in an identical mould, which, as a result of careful engineering, ensured that all the character blocks were cast with the same dimensions. The characters would then be arranged in wooden trays, inked, and paper placed on the surface under pressure of a hand operated press. One of the earliest dated examples of the output from this printing press was the Mainz Psalter, printed in 1457.

The style of type used was very close to that of the handwriting of the time. Even the abbreviations used, indicated by a short horizontal mark above the shortened word, were included in the printed text, so that the printed manuscripts would find acceptance with the readers, who would have only been used to hand-written documents previously. This conscious typographical decision suggests the earliest of considerations in respect of maintaining consistency and a standard approach to type design. Right from the beginnings of moveable type, it would seem, the reaction of the reader to the typeface was considered, and the decision to use characters which looked hand-written was, not surprisingly, strongly influenced by already familiar patterns and documents. This is still the case today, since we tend to use designs and typefaces which are contemporary. We are influenced by the magazines, newspapers and advertising designs and the typography which they use.

Type was cast by hand right up until the 19th century, with each character set manually to compose the words (see Figure 2.2). The metal blocks were laid in wooden trays called galleys and spacing between the lines of characters was added by inserting strips of lead; this gave rise to the term 'leading'. Large blocks with no characters cast on the surface were used to pad out the space between the last character on a line and the rest of the line itself, and these blocks were called 'quads'. This term also applies today, as quadding is meant to refer to the filling of space to the end of a line. If type was to be aligned to the right of the galley, quadding was

Figure 2.2   Hand Setting in Galleys

added on the left. If the type was to be centred on the line, the quadding was added equally to both sides.

Mechanisation

The mechanisation of typecasting was introduced by David Bruce in New York in 1838. This meant that characters could be cast on metal blocks more quickly, but to complement this acheivement, it was necessary to improve the setting process, so that the preparation of pages of type could also be speeded up. Previously, William Church, in Britain in 1822, patented a typesetting machine for this very purpose, but ultimately the machine which became universally used in the production of newspapers was the 'Linotype' (see Figure 2.3). This machine was patented by Ottmar Mergenthaler in the USA in 1884 and enabled a keyboard operator, working on a keyboard not unlike that of a typewriter, to select characters

Figure 2.3   An Early Linotype Composition Machine

which had been cast mechanically, and position them in lines of text. This line composition process is what gave the device its name, and although Linotype remains synonymous with typesetting today, setting line by line has now virtually disappeared.

Including Illustrations

Illustrations for inclusion in the printed text were still hand carved in wood or etched in metal. Pictures that were separate from the text could be produced by another method, called lithography, which is a technique now widely used for all types of printing, including text (see also Chapter 16).

TYPEFACES

By the time typesetting was being mechanised, there was already a wide range of typeface designs in use. Until the 1800s, nearly all typefaces were *serif* faces. A serif typeface is one in which each character has a short stroke at right angles or oblique to the main stroke or arm of the character (see Figure 2.4).

Figure 2.4   A Serif Character

Serif Typefaces

Serif characters were used in all forms of metal cast typesetting, whether for display work, such as headings or advertisements, or for book and document composition. A number of variants were in use and the names of the typefaces were often taken from the names of their designers. For example, one of the most famous serif typefaces, called 'Bodoni', was designed by Giambattista Bodoni, an Italian type founder, designer and printer who was born in Saluzzo, Northern Italy in 1740.

An important exception to this is probably one of the most well-known and popular serif typeface: 'Times', and one which you will almost certainly encounter when using desktop publishing. However, this almost universally accepted typeface was not introduced until the 20th century, by Stanley Morison, a consultant and typographic advisor to the Monotype Corporation, the Cambridge University Press and *The Times* newspaper of London. Morison was a dominant force in typography and printing from the 1920s and his design of Times New Roman, was probably one of the most successful typeface designs of the 20th century.

Italics

Among the serif typefaces are the italics. Italic typefaces are those in which the characters slant to the right. The italic style of typeface was developed around the 1500s. Aldus Manitus of Venice, probably one of the busiest printers in Europe at that time, adapted the cursive style of handwriting used in papal chancery and produced a metal type from it. This style was originally called *corsiva* (for cursive) or *cacellarsca* (chancery). Today, italic typefaces (as shown in this paragraph) are used for emphasis, but when they were first introduced, they were used to mimic the handwriting styles of manuscripts and, because of their shape, enabled more type to be set on a page than the normal, roman characters.

It is worth knowing that italics come in three different classes. There are those which are italic typefaces in their own right (modern examples include Chancery, designed by Hermman Zapf), those which are italic variations of a roman typeface (such as Times italic which looks like that used in this book), and Pseudo italics, ie those created by simply slanting a roman character. The difference between the latter two is that an italic variation of a typeface is actually a separate character shape to the roman version, as well as being slanted. Using modern electronic techniques, typefaces that do not have an italic equivalent of their own can be electronically slanted, which creates an italic-like appearance, but the shape and form of the characters does not otherwise alter.

Sans Serif Typefaces

'Sans serif' characters (those that do not have the serifs) did not appear in cast type until quite late in printing history. While sans serif characters had been used by signwriters for notices and on buidlings, because they were easier to draw, they did not appear in cast type until the 1800s. A capital roman character without serifs first appeared in a typeface in 1816, and was known as 'English Egyptian', and was used as a display typeface in advertising. By 1835, a lower case style of sans serif characters called 'Seven Lines Grotesque' emerged from a type foundry in London. It is said that the word 'grotesque', used to describe the typeface, reflected the reaction of the printers at that time to the type design. Well-known sans serif typefaces include designs like Gill, Univers, Helvetica, Avant Garde and Franklin Gothic, among many others.

THE INFLUENCE OF TYPEFACES

Apart from the development of typefaces, the design and use of them in typography has been influenced by the art and ideas of the times in which they were used. Apart from the typefaces used in general settting requirements for printing books, posters, newspapers, etc, many new typestyles emerged as a result of commercial developments. Today, typefaces are designed especially for advertising, corporate images, signs and displays, and you can see how these have changed simply by looking at the style of printed material throughout the last decade or so. It is perhaps an indication of the power of typographical design that we can instantly recognise an 'old' advertisement; simply because the design, layout, typeface and illustrations used dates it, compared to modern style advertisements (see Figure 2.5).

The history of typography is always being made. There is no

Figure 2.5   Advertisement from the 1960s

point at which typography 'arrived', as it has always been an evolving and fluid combination of technical and artistic skills, reflecting the influences of the era.

3   The Nature of Type

Type, as far as desktop publishing is concerned, refers to the form of the characters, whether they are letters, numbers or symbols. Unlike previous type forms, which were produced by physically shaping a block, electronic methods of describing type offer considerably more flexibility in the possible combinations of style and visual effects that may be obtained. This is partly due to the 'mechanics' of the process in that fine control can be afforded to the shape of a character when produced electronically.

RESOLUTION

Desktop publishing systems and modern digital phototypesetting machines share very similar methods of type description. The characters are made up of a pattern of dots, or pixels. These are very fine dots indeed, and can therefore provide a very clear outline definition. The output device of a desktop publishing system reproduces a character by placing dots in the shape of the character's image, and the finer the dots that can be used to do this, the sharper will be the character's image at the edges. This sharpness of type is called the *resolution*.

A 'high resolution' means that a device is capable of outputting a large number of fine dots in a given area, usually referred to in inches. For example, a typical laser printer may be capable of reproducing 300 dots per inch (written as 300 dpi); a sufficiently high resolution to provide adequate quality in type for most printing requirements. On the other hand, a phototypesetter may be able to reproduce 1500 dots per inch or more, and consequently produces a far sharper and more cleanly defined character outline. Such a high resolution as this is important for high quality print work, eg glossy magazines, advertising, promotional material, etc. The resolution measurement is sometimes given in square inches, so a 300 dpi would in fact yield 90,000 dots per square inch.

Formation of Characters

To take a closer look at the formation of characters in desktop publishing typesetting systems, we need to enlarge part of a single character, as shown in Figure 3.1, below.

Figure 3.1   Enlarged Character Form

This illustrates how the dots make up a curved edge, and indicates that the 'smoothness' of form depends upon how fine the dots are. The finer the dots, and more densely packed they are in a given space, the nearer the edge will become to being a true curve. The reason that phototypesetters have much higher resolution than laser printers is twofold. First, as the name implies, phototypesetting involves a photographic process. An image of a character is projected onto a light-sensitive paper (ie the character's image is 'exposed') and this paper is then processed chemically, to produce a black and white reproduction known as a *bromide*. The photosensitive paper is very smooth, sometimes slightly glossy, and can accurately reproduce fine images on its surface. Paper used in laser printers, on the other hand, is not so smooth and this restricts the level of accuracy with which the image can be reproduced. (The paper needs to be slightly rough to take the toner particles as described below.) Also the way in which paper is transported through the device inhibits accuracy further.

The second aspect which differentiates between the resolution of laser printers and phototypesetters is that laser printers use *toner* (like that used in dry paper copiers), the toner powder, however fine it may seem, puts a physical limit on the resolution that may be obtained using this form of technology. Phototypesetting, on the other hand, produces its image photochemically, and is more able to provide fine images.

Both technologies produce the character's image using dots, however, and the placement of dots is under the control of the computer. For each physical location on a page on which a dot may be printed, the output device, be it a phototypesetter or laser printer, receives a signal which indicates whether a dot is to be produced or not. Such a simple process is ideal for the binary technology of computers, and thus the technology of desktop publishing permits the reproduction of text and graphics on the same page using the same process.

Raster Lines

Although the process of reproducing character images, as described previously, is based on dots, many output devices in fact manipulate the images as vertical lines made of a series of single dots. For example, a single vertical row of dots, if enlarged, might look like the illustration in Figure 3.2.

These vertical lines of dots are called *raster lines* and devices which process them are called raster image processing devices. A raster line, comprises a vertical row of dots, and the number of raster lines that can be printed in a given space is determined by

Figure 3.2   Enlarged Section of a Line

the dot resolution of the device. Raster processing has advantages which are described later, that enable certain effects to be produced.

TYPEFACE DESCRIPTIONS

The design of a particular typeface can be described electronically. Type information in desktop publishing systems is provided in many ways: on disk, in the printer's own memory, on cartridge, etc. In each case, the type information describes a basic outline of a particular character set for a given design of typeface. This information can be used to produce different sizes of the same typeface, and to produce variations of the face (italics, bold, etc). When a character is entered at the keyboard, it is effectively electronically translated into the appropriate shape or form of the chosen typeface. When a different typeface is selected, a different set of instructions apply to the outline of the character, and hence a new appearance of the character results.

If the character's size is changed, one of two processes may occur. With some laser printing devices, a change in size is effected by using a different set of outline instructions (peculiar to PCL laser printers — those which require type information to be loaded into the printer's memory from store on disk or cartridge). For devices which use a page description language (such as PostScript), the typesize can be changed by 'scaling up' the raster lines, or dots, to automatically provide a new size; mathematically calculating the new proportions. This scaling ability enables the size of characters to be altered by very fine degrees and does not put the same kind of limit on the maximum size of a character as applies to a PCL device.

Condensed and Expanded Characters

Using this computer-controlled dot process enables electronic means of typesetting to produce effects easily on a standard typeface outline. Raster lines may be added or removed from a character's form to electronically reduce or expand the width of the character. If you examine the enlarged example in Figure 3.3, you can see that a character can be condensed by removing an evenly spaced number of raster lines. In effect, the character is made thinner, but the outline description remains the same, ie the typeface does not alter, only the style.

This letter 'I' is diagrammatically represented as raster lines

By removing lines, the character is made proportionally thinner

Figure 3.3   Raster Condensing

Should the opposite effect be desired, raster lines may be added to the normal number of lines which described the character, thus expanding its width. Note that in both cases, the height of the character is not affected, only the width. Using this kind of image manipulation offers the typesetter scope to provide variation in style of lettering without having to change the typeface, which might otherwise be detrimental to the quality and appearance of the finished article. Such adjustments also help to fit headings and other large type into a predefined space, which would not normally be wide enough for the characters. Conversely, adjustments can also help to fill out white space if the characters are suitably expanded.

The effects produced by adding or removing raster lines are not normally found on PCL printer devices, but can easily be obtained using page description languages, such as PostScript, and are nearly always available on phototypesetting devices. Changing the character width is known as changing the *set width* of the type; this is mentioned again in later chapters of this book.

TYPEFACES AND THE PRINTING PROCESS

Typefaces can be provided for use in desktop publishing systems in a number of ways. Since typefaces are essentially a form of software, they may be supplied on disk. Modern laser printers usually include a number of 'built in' typefaces. In fact they are software descriptions of typefaces stored in a special sort of memory which remains permanently held in the printer. Whenever a typeface is chosen for a particular printing job, the information about how the typeface should look may be available in the printer, if not, it will need to be supplied in some other way.

Typeface information can be sent to a printer from the computer that is carrying out the desktop publishing operation. The descriptions of the outlines of the typeface are stored on disk and are known as *soft fonts*. When a document which requires a particular typeface is to be printed, the information about the font is sent to the printer's own memory so that it acts as if it were built into the printer itself. Such typefaces usually require the printer to have a large amount of memory available, since the printer must store the font information while at the same time handling the text and graphics that may be in the document itself. Soft fonts provide a useful way of providing font information for a printer and for expanding upon the built-in typefaces. Standard digital phototypesetters use disk-based fonts in this way, and each disk may contain information about a complete type family — roman, italic, bold and book versions of the same font.

Some laser printers make use of cartridges on which typeface information is stored. The cartridge is plugged into the printer and acts as if it were part of the printer's own memory. By keeping fonts on cartridge, the appropriate typeface can be supplied for any given job simply by plugging in the right cartridge.

With the advent of modern page description languages, such as PostScript, the font capabilities of many desktop publishing systems has been greatly enhanced. Rather than the printer storing a specific font outline, it has its own programmable software which can receive instructions from the computer about how a typeface is to look. Although PostScript laser printers store many details of fonts readily available for use, (ie the printer already knows the outline of a set of typefaces) any other typeface can be provided by the printer simply receiving the right instructions from the computer in the PostScript language. Thus desktop publishing packages can themselves provide information about new typefaces to the printer and these can be used as if they were resident. This method also makes typeface processing much quicker than other forms of font control, with the added advantage that the same processing language is used to print graphic images as well as text, so that an entire page containing both a mixture of typefaces and graphic images can be processed as one unit (hence the name 'page printers'). Page processing can be significantly quicker than other types of laser printer processing.

Today, new typefaces are constantly being designed. They are still hand-drawn at first by skilled typographical designers and graphic artists, and if a complete set of characters is designed, it may become a new typeface family in its own right. Transferring hand-drawn designs to electronic form for use in typesetters is performed using a digitising process (rather like a scanner in many ways) which converts the solid image into one that may be 'described' electronically as a series of dots or raster lines. Once the information for a typeface is encoded, it may be mathematically enlarged or reduced to produce typefaces of different sizes, and other qualities, such as boldness, can also be electronically manipulated.

4   Typefaces and Typestyles

GENERAL

Typographers classify typefaces using names which may describe groups of faces or individual faces. The group names, which form part of a British Standard specification, are not likely to be encountered by the average desktop publishing system user, since they are classification names used strictly in design and typographical circles, for example: 'Humanist', 'Garald', 'Transitional', 'Didone', etc. It will be more likely that, as a desktop publishing system user, you will encounter typeface names which are specific to the type family alone, for example: 'Garamond', 'Bembo', 'Plantin', 'Univers', etc. There are many typefaces — over 2000 of them — each with their own characteristics of design and form, usually named after the designer of the typeface. Many typefaces of different names may, at first sight, seem very similar. Indeed, to the naked eye, some may be almost indistinguishable, except, perhaps, for some slight differences in particular letters or numbers.

These typefaces may also vary slightly in appearance according to the original supplier of the typeface, even though two faces with different names may be virtually indistinguishable. One such example is the variation that can be seen of the popular 'Times' typeface (not surprisingly used on *The Times* newspaper). This most widely used typeface, and one almost certainly available on every conceivable desktop publishing system, has a vast range of uses from bookwork to general documents, reports, leaflets, adverts, etc. One variation of the name includes 'Dutch' (in which this book was typeset). Similarly, 'Helvetica' is another popular face used on desktop publishing systems, and one name variant of this typeface is 'Swiss' ('Helvetica' is a Swiss-designed typeface and the name comes from the Latin name for Switzerland, which was Helvetia).

These two examples, 'Times' and 'Helvetica', introduce the difference between two major classes of typefaces — serif and sans serif. These are explained in this chapter, along with the reason why these two particular classes are important in respect of the design of the printed word. There are many factors which affect the apparent 'legibility' of a typeface, and you should understand that when one refers to type being legible, it is in the sense of the *readability* of the text, not the comprehension of it (ie ability to understand it). Typographically speaking, ensuring the legibility of a publication by choosing the appropriate typeface has to do with considering who the reader of the printed material will be and the purpose of the printed matter. So, for example, the typeface used on a wedding invitation may look attractive by being 'flowery' and decorative, yet still be practical for the purpose of conveying the invitation. However, the same typeface would be an inappropriate choice for a road sign which must convey information clearly, and be instantly readable, without ambiguity, from a reasonable distance.

The selection of a typeface should be a conscious effort, based upon a number of considerations. The following two classes of typeface (serif and sans serif) come in a wide selection of styles. Since the advent of phototypesetting, the variety of typefaces has increased considerably. This is due to the fact that, previously, new faces had to be cut in metal, a labour-intensive job, but are now produced by the process of digitising from flat artwork.

SERIF TYPEFACES

As mentioned earlier, serif typefaces are ones which use short lines drawn at right angles to or obliquely across the ends of stems and arms of letters. Figure 4.1 shows a selection of serif typefaces, including some of the most popular used for general publishing

Aster Medium
Aster Italic
Aster Bold
Aster Bold (Slanted)

Baskerville Roman
Baskerville Italic
Baskerville Bold
Baskerville Bold Italic

Bembo Medium
Bembo Italic
Bembo Bold
Bembo Bold Italic

Bodoni Medium
Bodoni Italic
Bodoni Bold
Bodoni Bold Italic
Bodoni Black
Bodoni Black (Slanted)
Bodoni Black Condensed
Bodoni Black Condensed (Slanted)

Century Old Style Medium
Century Old Style Italic
Century Old Style Bold
Century Old Style Bold (Slanted)

Case Fraction (Serif)

Figure 4.1   A Selection of Serif Typefaces

and bookwork. They include most classes of typeface used for bookwork and continuous setting, where readability is important over long passages. It is generally considered unwise to mix different serif faces together in the same publication, and is usually pointless as many of them are very similar in appearance, certainly more so than the different sans serif faces. Serif typefaces are also used for display type.

The parts of a letter have special names, and while these are not normally referred to in most desktop publishing systems, you may come across them at a future date. Figure 4.2 shows some letters and their parts with corresponding names, and also the names given to the different types of serif.

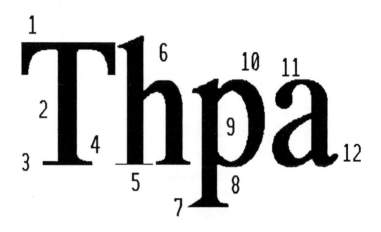

Key:	1	Serif	7	Wedge serif
	2	Main stem	8	Descender
	3	Slab serif	9	Counter
	4	Bracketed serif	10	Bowl
	5	Hairline serif	11	Loop
	6	Ascender	12	Finial

Figure 4.2   Parts of Letters

SANS SERIF TYPEFACES

San serif typefaces are, by definition, those without serifs, and are mainly used in display work. In desktop publishing you will probably find that you use sans serif typefaces for headings, captions, figures and tables, while leaving serif typefaces for body text of longer publications.

There is no hard and fast rule about this, however, and some instruction manuals or brochures may use a sans serif typeface for the body text, which often gives an overall impression of a 'clean and simple' looking page. It is perhaps ironic that a carefully spaced page of sans serif text can look as if it will be easier to read than one set in serif, at least at first glance. In fact, serif typefaces can be read more easily, and are less tiresome over longer passages of text.

Some examples of well known sans serif typefaces are shown in Figure 4.3. The variety of style in sans serif is quite acute, probably due to the fact that they are more widely used for display type, on posters, signs, etc.

SELECTING THE TYPEFACE

Why are certain typefaces chosen in preference to others? The answer to this question will always be a subjective one. Decisions about the right typeface for a particular job tend to come down to a mixture of common sense and personal preference. Typefaces may be selected that are appealing for most publication jobs and suitable for use as part of a corporate identity. In other words, a particular typeface becomes part of the 'house style' so that any publication from the organisation carries the chosen typeface as part of the organisation's identity. Some typefaces look more elegant than others. The 'Times' typeface is very practical, but also rather boring. It carries an air of authority, because it is formal. For publications such as books, important documents and official publications, such a typeface will probably seem most suitable — a conservative choice, that does not distract the reader from the content of the material.

Avant Garde Gothic Light
Avant Garde Gothic Light (Slanted)
Avant Garde Gothic Medium
Avant Garde Gothic Med. (Slanted)
Avant Garde Gothic Bold
Avant Garde Gothic Bold (Slanted)

Gill Sans Light
Gill Sans Light (Slanted)
Gill Sans Medium
Gill Sans Medium (Slanted)
Gill Sans Bold
Gill Sans Bold (Slanted)
Gill Sans Extra Bold
Gill Sans Extra Bold (Slanted)

Helvetica Light
Helvetica Light (Slanted)
Helvetica Medium
Helvetica Medium (Slanted)
Helvetica Bold
Helvetica Bold (Slanted)
Helvetica Black
Helvetica Black (Slanted)
Helvetica Light Condensed
Helvetica Light Condensed (Slanted)
Helvetica Medium Condensed
Helvetica Medium Condensed (Slanted)
Helvetica Bold Condensed

Figure 4.3   A Selection of Sans Serif Typefaces

Some typefaces have more character in them, and may enhance the publication in which they are used, provided they are used with restraint. A quality sales brochure, for example, may have a better appearance if set in an attractive typeface, such as 'Benguiat', than it would if set in 'Times', but it all depends upon the image one is trying to portray. The more flamboyant the typeface is in appearance, the more careful one should be in the use of it. It is so easy to 'overcook' a publication by including either too many typefaces, or by the over-use of a decorative font.

With experience you should find that you will be able to identify those typefaces which are most appropriate for your requirements. Those using desktop publishing for the first time, especially if they have access to the wide range of typefaces provided by PostScript systems, tend to go through a period of playing with several different typefaces for all kinds of publications. Unless you are using desktop publishing in a service role (ie you are producing artwork for clients, where selection may be important), you are better finding two or three typefaces for general use, for example, one sans serif and a couple of serif faces, and sticking to them.

Type Variations

Do not forget that there is variety within the type family of any given typeface. Each form has its own name, and may relate to the *weight* of the typeface (ie the thickness of line). A bold face is usually easily recognised simply because its characters look thicker and 'darker'. But there is often more than one form of bold, there may be *medium-bold*, *bold* and *ultra-bold*, all of which will be heavier versions of a particular typeface than its normal roman (ie neither bold nor italic) form, but of progressively heavier weights. The roman type itself may be available in a number of forms: *light*, *medium-light*, *medium*, *book*, etc. In this context, the word 'book' refers to the weight of the typeface and not to the other use of the word as in 'book face', which is just another way of identifying a serif typeface. These different weights of type each have their own particular applications. Combining the right weights of a typeface may be important. For example, a medium typeface when combined with light-bold may result in the reader having difficulty in distinguishing the bold from the roman type, and this difference may become even less apparent in the printing process.

The selection of typeface can also be a matter of space, since the height of the lower case part of a character (known as the x-height) can vary from typeface to typeface. Some typefaces need more vertical space than others so as not to appear too crowded. The set width of characters also affects the amount of type that can be fitted onto a line. Choosing a typeface for fitting into a particular space requires knowledge of different font widths, and is therefore a task for the more experienced designer, (there is more on copy fitting later in the book). However, it is worth bearing in mind that typeface style can affect the amount of text that can be fitted into a given space, so you do not necessarily need to rely entirely on a change of typesize or line spacing in order to make text fit.

Using sans serif typefaces for headings in conjunction with a serif body text for the bulk of a document is often a preferred formula to simply one font selection. Sans serif faces can be used in great variety for headings by expanding, condensing and ranging right, using a mixture of weights, for example. The variety, in this respect, is usually far more apparent than in serif faces. Typefaces such as 'Helvetica' and 'Univers' with their mathematically accurate character forms, offer designers considerable flexibility in alignment and presentation of display type, and you should experiment with these typefaces for the headings of your documents.

Figure 4.4   Evocative Typefaces

Typefaces and style variations can be used to create a mood or feeling in a publication. Desktop publishing systems often provide special versions of a given typeface not normally part of the type family's characteristics (for example, outline typefaces or shadowed text as shown in Figure 4.4).

SELECTION OF TYPE

In the early stages of the development of your typographical awareness, it is sometimes helpful to follow certain suggestions for the selection of typefaces, styles, sizes, spacing, etc, until such time as you feel that you can appreciate the consequences of certain decisions about these factors. Look at other examples of similar types of publication to the one you are producing on your desktop publishing system. Use examples that you feel comfortable with, and if you find a particular typeface or style that you like, use that typeface or one similar to it.

For example, when setting book text, it is probably best to start by using a serif typeface like 'Times' or 'Garamond' at around 11 or 12pt. You will probably find that most books use a typeface of similar size and design (at least they do not vary greatly). If you are setting a letter heading or similar design, your choice of typeface will be more important, and so more time should be spent comparing the possibilities of the whole range of typefaces that your system has to offer. If you are limited to a choice of 'Times' and 'Helvetica' only, then your decision will naturally be simpler, but you should still experiment with the weights, sizes and styles of these typefaces, as well as their position on the page.

Look for ways of expanding your typeface choices if your desktop publishing system's offerings are limited, and especially if you are not happy with the ones available. But remember that your selection of typeface should be kept to a minimum using the designs that have a wide application within the scope of the work you are likely to undertake.

If you think carefully about your typeface selections on each job, and spend some time trying a few alternative styles using the

ANNOUNCING OUR LATEST
PRODUCT FOR THE 1990s...

A TURBO-POWERED, 6 CYLINDER, FUEL
INJECTED LAWN MOWER!

DCF Products are pleased to invite our
valued distributors to the launch of this
new product. We will be holding a special
demonstration and presentation lunch at
the Imperial Hotel, Wisbeach.

To book your place on the luncheon, *call Louise on 0763
89782, and quote your distributor reference.*

If you would like more information about our new product range before the launch, contact your area sales
representative.

This bulletin is issue 9003, July, 1990.
DFC Products Limited, Wells Next the Sea, Norfolk.
Tel. 0763 89782. Fax. 0763 44121.

Figure 4.5   Bad Selection of Typefaces

same typeface, you should begin to feel comfortable with one or
two particular selections. In this way, you can develop your own
house style and introduce consistency of appearance throughout
the various products of your system. In so many examples of desktop publishing output, a bad typeface selection stands out more
than any other aspect of bad design (see Figure 4.5), and this is a

reflection of the power of type design to influence the overall appearance of a document. It is necessary, therefore, to choose a typeface carefully, particularly when presented with the ever widening range that is now available due to the improvements in electronic publishing technology.

5   Size and Spacing

Size and spacing of type are discussed together because they are closely related. The space that is given between two lines of type also depends upon the style of the typeface, to a certain extent, and so this will be considered too. When you select a particular typesize, your decision will be the result of a number of considerations, such as what the text is to be used for and whether it is a heading or the body of a document; this will have a direct bearing on the choice of the most appropriate spacing.

TYPESIZE

People often confuse the size of a typeface with the actual dimensions of the printed characters, so the smaller the characters look, the smaller the typesize; this is only partly true, as you will see. In most desktop publishing systems, the size of the typeface will be quantified by its *point size*. The point (which is used with the abbreviation 'pt') is the basic unit of measurement in typography, and most other dimensions used in printing are derived from this one measurement. The point is actually 1/72nd of an inch and is used for the measurement of spacing, as well as typefaces.

When describing a typeface as being 12pt or 24pt, for example, the measurement is traditionally based upon the size of the metal body of the type, ie as the character would be cast on a metal block for printing purposes. This may be different from the *apparent size* of the character, depending upon whether the form (shape) of the characters affects the height of the ascenders and descenders. Figure 5.1, below, illustrates this.

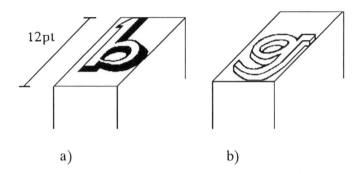

a)   b)

Figure 5.1   Point Size Measurement

Note that in a) the character 'b' has an ascender which goes to the top of the metal block, and in b) the character 'g' has a descender which goes to the bottom of the type block. The point size of the typeface is actually measured from the top of the metal block to the bottom (known as the body size). Now look at Figure 5.2, below.

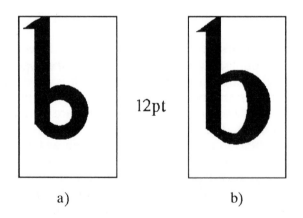

a)   b)

Figure 5.2   Body Size of Type

Note that the letter on block b) appears larger than the letter on

the block a). This is due to a difference in the design of the
typeface, which results in a) appearing to be a smaller typesize
than b) even though they are in fact both 12pt typefaces.

Another measurement comes into play which describes this
apparent size difference, and this is called the *x-height*. The x-
height is the measurement of the height of the lower case character, excluding the ascender and the descender as shown in Figure
5.3.

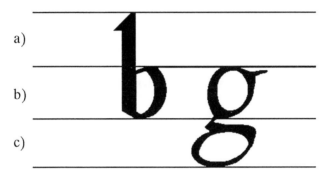

a) ascender height   b) x-height   c) descender height

Figure 5.3   x-Height

If the x-height is smaller, the apparent size of the typeface will
be smaller. When typefaces with a low x-height are put alongside
those of a tall x-height, the impression given is that one typeface
is a larger point size than the other. Only by measuring from the
top of the tallest character in the typeface to the bottom of the
descender can the true typesize be measured.

When using a desktop publishing system, however, you can
confirm the typesize by referring to the information provided on
the screen about the particular typeface in use. The size of the
typeface can be changed, simply by selecting a new point size. The
importance of knowing about the true typesize measurement and
x-height, is that, should you select a typeface which has a low x-
height compared with other typefaces available on your system,

you may otherwise be fooled into thinking that you are using a
smaller typesize.

In some cases, a typeface may have ascenders and descenders
which do not reach the limits of the body size in points. For
example, Figure 5.4, below, shows three characters in a typefaces
where this is the case.

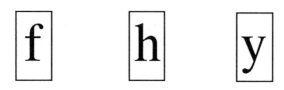

Figure 5.4   Short Ascenders and Descenders

Only the capital letter goes to the top of the body size. The area
left between the descender of the typeface and the bottom of the
block creates an amount of space which not only affects the appearance of the type design, but which would have an effect on the
choice of the appropriate spacing.

So spacing, which is the second subject of this chapter, can be
affected by the design of the typeface, and whether or not the
spacing looks right; this might depend upon the height of the ascenders and descenders of a typeface, as well as the typesize itself.

SPACING

Spacing in typography affects many qualities of a publication.
There are many spacing considerations that can determine
whether a section of text looks right on paper. Each of the spacing
attributes may be altered in isolation, or together to affect the
appearance of the publication. There are three main categories
relating to spacing type and most desktop publishing systems cater
for all of them, though the degree of control afforded to each may
vary. These categories are:

— spacing between characters;

— spacing between words;

— spacing between lines.

(There is also the spacing around a block of text, including the margins of the paper). All these affect the appearance of a typeface when they are changed. The spacing between characters comes under a special term, known as *kerning* — which is a method of space adjustment used particularly with large type and a special subject that is covered in the following chapter. In this chapter, we will discuss the space between words and the line spacing.

Word Spacing

Word spacing is something which is peculiar to typesetting as opposed to typewriting. A typewriter uses an even amount of space for each letter or character, thus a letter 'i' takes up the same width on the paper as a letter 'm', though, physically, the 'm' is much wider. In addition, the width of the space character used between words is equal to all the other characters, and so word spacing is always even. In the case of word processing, the letter widths may also be the same as a typewriter, though many modern word processing systems now provide much more flexibility. Changing the space between words allows a line of characters to be spread to a right-hand margin so that all the letters at the right of a block of text are aligned in the same way as they are on the left (this paragraph, for example, is typeset in this manner). As words are added to a line, the amount of space between the words is constantly being adjusted by the desktop publishing system, until no more words can be fitted on the line. This process is known as *justification* and is described in Chapter 7.

Word spacing can be adjusted manually using three kinds of space control: the *thin space*, the *en space* and the *em space*. The actual width of these three spaces is dependent upon the point size of the typeface. This is important since many people think that an em space is always the same size. However, it is usually based on the typeface size in points, thus a 32pt em would be created for a 32pt typeface. An en space is half an em space, and a thin space is either 1/4 or 1/3 an em space.

In any typeface, the widths of characters are proportional to one another (i.e. letter 'i' uses proportionally less space than a letter 'm') and this proportionality remains the same, even if the point size is changed. By keeping a relative unit of measurement between different point sizes, an em space for a 36pt typeface may be made up of relative units of 2 points, and in 72pt would be made up of relative units of 4 points (ie twice the width). These special spaces that can be manually added between words are called *fixed spaces*, because they remain in place regardless of the width of a line of type or the number of words on the line.

Line Spacing

The space between lines of type has traditionally been known as *leading*. It is still referred to by this name (as well as 'line spacing'), even though the term originates from the days of manual typesetting where lines of metal blocks of type were separated by strips of lead. The thickness of the strip of lead determined the amount of space between lines of type and thus the term is still used on desktop publishing systems for the value of the line space. The distance between lines of type is usually measured in points, however, the actual distance is not measured between the ascenders and descenders of a typeface, but between the baselines. This is because the ascender and descender lengths can vary, as explained earlier in this chapter.

The baseline is the line which corresponds to the base of the normal character, disregarding the descender (see Figure 5.5). When you measure from the baseline of one character to the baseline of another on the next line down in a paragraph, you can determine the value of the line spacing. While most typefaces are measured in points, many desktop publishing systems allow you to measure in inches, millimetres, centimetres, picas or even fractions of a normal line space, according to your preference. The last of these involves specifying whether you want a full line space (calculated for you automatically), half a line space, or a double-line space, etc. Such a system is rather limited, however, and much finer control over line spacing is usually preferable.

Figure 5.5 The Baseline Position

The amount of leading used should depend upon the point size of the typeface chosen. Some desktop publishing systems will calculate the optimum for you, but there is usually a facility which will enable you to override the default values for spacing. If you consider the traditional form of manual typesetting where metal blocks carry the character shapes, should a character with a descender which reaches the bottom of the block be placed directly above a character on the line below which has an ascender, the two characters would meet with no space between them, as shown in Figure 5.6.

$$p \atop h$$

Figure 5.6   Ascender and Descender meet

This is a situation which is best avoided. The term used to describe setting with no additional spacing above that of the depth of the type size is called solid setting. By nature of their design, some typefaces (those whose ascenders and descenders do not reach the full depth of the type's body size), may be successfully set solid, and thus make maximum use of the vertical space available on the paper. Under normal circumstances, however, it is best to follow the 'rules' of leading shown in Table 5.1.

Strict adherence to these rules is not absolutely essential, but you will find that generally they describe values for leading that provide a clear, readable setting which does not look unduly cramped or overspaced. Some desktop publishing systems refer to leading as a percentage of the actual point size of the typeface. For example specifying the leading as 110% of the point size would ensure that the value of the leading (whether in points or millimetres) is proportionally 10% greater than that of the typesize. So, a typeface of 10pt would be set with a line spacing of 11pt. This would be described as setting '10 on 11'.

Type Size	Minimum Leading	Optimum Leading	Maximum Leading
6pt	Solid	1pt	1pt
7pt	Solid	1pt	1.5pt
8pt	Solid	1.5pt	2pt
9pt	Solid	2pt	3pt
10pt	Solid	2pt	3pt
11pt	1pt	2pt	3pt
12pt	2pt	3pt	4pt
14pt	3pt	4pt	6pt
16pt	4pt	4pt	6pt
18pt	5pt	4pt	6pt

Note: Solid means no leading

Table 5.1   Recommended Values for Leading

In addition to leading used to add space between the baselines of a typeface, some desktop publishing systems allow you to use negative leading. This actually reduces the distance between the baselines of two lines of text so that the lines actually overlap. This may be used in cases where a section of text is set in capital letters such that there are no descenders, and hence the space that would otherwise be used by the ascenders can be used with negative leading to reduce the distance between the characters on each line. Try experimenting with different values of leading to see how the changes can affect the appearance of a publication. You will, of course, see a greater effect on a paragraph of text than on one or two lines, and Figure 5.7 shows some of the changes in appear-

ance which different values bring about on text of the same type
size.

'Go placidly amid the noise and haste and remember what peace
there may be in silence. As far as possible without surrender, be
on good terms with all persons. Speak your truth quietly and
clearly and listen to others; even the dull and the ignorant, they
too have their story. Avoid loud and aggressive persons, they are
vexations to the spirit. If you compare yourselves to others you
will become vain and bitter, for, always, there will be greater and
lesser persons than yourself. . .'

a) 10pt on 10pt (solid)

'Go placidly amid the noise and haste and remember what peace
there may be in silence. As far as possible without surrender, be
on good terms with all persons. Speak your truth quietly and
clearly and listen to others; even the dull and the ignorant, they
too have their story. Avoid loud and aggressive persons, they are
vexations to the spirit. If you compare yourselves to others you
will become vain and bitter, for, always, there will be greater and
lesser persons than yourself. . .'

b) 10pt on 11pt

'Go placidly amid the noise and haste and remember what peace
there may be in silence. As far as possible without surrender, be
on good terms with all persons. Speak your truth quietly and
clearly and listen to others; even the dull and the ignorant, they
too have their story. Avoid loud and aggressive persons, they are
vexations to the spirit. If you compare yourselves to others you
will become vain and bitter, for, always, there will be greater and
lesser persons than yourself. . .'

c) 10pt on 12pt

Figure 5.7   Leading Comparisons

6 Multiple Columns

One of the features which sets desktop publishing apart from word processing is the ability to set out your text in multiple columns. This enables you to create a variety of effects, which can be simply aesthetic or have a practical advantage. For example, it is often possible to fit much more text onto a page using columns (like newspapers and magazines) because it is more readable than it would otherwise be if spread across the width of a page.

Part of your design process will be choosing when to use columns and deciding on their appropriate width. Generally speaking, the larger the typeface you use, the wider the columns should be. You will need to consider the paper size and, therefore, how many columns look acceptable to ensure that a balance is achieved between the space on the paper and that used for text and graphics. The space between and around columns should also be considered. Increasing white space around columns can serve many purposes. For example, extra white space may be used to provide room for notes, especially on training documents and course notes, or simply for the purpose of giving distinction to the appearance of a document.

The widths of the columns in a document do not have to be equal, although this is generally the case with newspapers and magazines. Using columns of differing widths can help to create interest in the overall appearance, and can be seen in books where one column is used for illustrations and associated captions, or where a narrow column of text is used to introduce and support the main story, which is contained in a wider column alongside (see Figure 6.1). If using columns of varying width, it is probably

In the example above, a two-column format has been used, with a wide central margin to offset the columns from the binding. This may be useful where the binding of a document is not particularly flexible (such as perfect binding) and it is therefore not easy to open the pages flat.

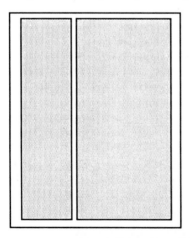

This page layout also uses a two column format, but with the first column narrower for the purpose of creating a more interesting layout. This could be used for illustrations and captions or simply for placing headings, offset from the text in the right column, so that they are easily identifiable.

Figure 6.1   Possible Column Layouts

best to restrict yourself to two columns, and certainly no more than three. The more columns you have on a page, the more important it is for them to be balanced, otherwise the page will look quite clumsy.

Apart from choosing the columns and their widths, you should consider whether to justify the text within the columns. As a general guide, justified columns tend to look more formal and allow more text to be included in the space provided. However, the narrower the column, the greater the likelihood of large word spaces appearing or the excessive use of hyphenation, in order to fit the text into the column and align it on the right. The column widths of broadsheet newspapers give you an example of this (see Figure 6.2). Magazines tend to have wider columns and on the whole are justified.

> Lorem ipsum dolor sit amet, con secetuer adipsicing elit, sed diam nonnumy nibh eeuismod tempor inci dunt ut labore et dolore magna ali quam erat volupat. Ut wisi enim ad minim veniam, quis nostrud exerci tation ullamcorper suscipt laboris nisl ut aliquip ex ea commodo consequat. Duis autem vel eum irure dolor in henderit in vulputate esse consequat. Lorem ipsum dolor sit amet, con secetuer adipsicing elit, sed diam nonnumy nibh eeuismod tempor inci dunt ut

Text in the above column has been justified. Each line ends at the same point and spacing between words is adjusted accordingly. Hyphenation is used to reduce the size of word spaces to an acceptable degree where long words do not otherwise fit at the end of a line.

Figure 6.2   A Justified Column

The decision about the amount of spacing to be used between columns and margins will depend on the amount of copy you need to include on the page, as well as the size and style of the typeface and the paper size and shape. The white space around columns helps to focus the eye on the type area, this is because our eyes are accustomed to certain conventions. A marked deviation from convention is likely to interrupt the flow of the reading and certainly, you should avoid changing column widths and margins too often within a given publication, as this tends to unbalance the document's page layout and consistency is lost. The publication could then give the impression of being a compendium of smaller publications, rather than separate stories.

The space at the bottom of a column of text on a page should be larger than at the top, otherwise the type in the column area has the appearance of falling out of the page (see Figure 6.3). Space between columns should always be smaller than that of the margins at the edge of the paper, so that the columns do not appear disconnected. The page layout should appear to be a single entity.

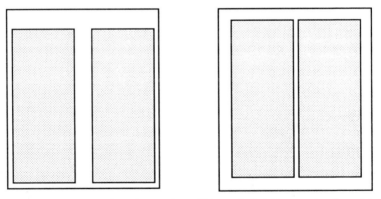

These two examples show the effect of the amount of space used around and between columns. The example on the left has the top margin larger than the bottom, and the column spacing (gutter) wider than the left and right margins. The example on the right has a more balanced appearance.

Figure 6.3   Examples of Column Spacing

As a general rule, the narrower the columns in a document, the more important it is to use a smaller typeface. The overall look of a block of text is sometimes referred to as the 'colour' of the layout. The more dense the text in a given space, the 'blacker' the page and the less dense, the 'greyer' it is. The combination of correct line spacing and typesize will ensure that the page does not look either too dark and dense or too light and excessively spacey. It is a common mistake not to adjust the leading on desktop publishing systems when a smaller point size is chosen. Even though some systems will do this for you automatically, you may need to make a further adjustment in order to make the spacing look correct (a table of line spacing suggestions is given in Chapter 5).

All these factors, are important for page layout and become magnified when used in a columnar format. The narrower width makes more demands upon the designer to ensure that type and spacing are suitable.

GUTTERS AND DIVIDERS

Desktop publishing systems vary in the manner in which they handle gutters — the space between columns of text in a multiple column format. However, most systems allow you to specify the column width and will calculate the gutter space according to the page width or type area and the number of columns required. If not, then you will need to specify the width of the gutter, which should always be the same between any two columns.

The use of a line separating the columns is often employed, particularly if the document is a newsletter or bulletin-style publication. There is a tendency, however, to place column dividers between all columns and, indeed, some desktop publishing systems do this automatically. If you look at a newspaper or magazine, you will notice that, in most cases, the column divider is only used between columns of text belonging to different stories. Provided the correct typesize and spacing has been selected, and the margins and column widths chosen with care, there should be no reason to separate the columns of text with a divider simply for the sake of it. The columns should be easily distinguishable on the page, therefore, use a line as a story divider only, so that it is clear to the reader exactly where the boundaries of a given article are, as shown in Figure 6.4.

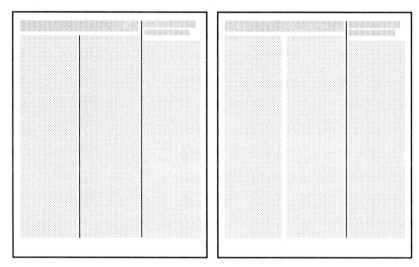

These two examples show the use of column dividers. The example on the left uses column dividers between every column, although there are only two stories on the page. The example on the right illustrates the use of a single divider between the two stories.

Figure 6.4   Use of Column Dividers

The weight of the line used as a column divider should not be excessive in relation to the weight of the typeface. A half-point line, or even hairline if your printer will manage it, should be all that is necessary. Be careful to accurately centre the column divider in the space between the columns if you are adding it manually as a vertical rule.

COLUMN HEADINGS

As figure 6.4 shows, column headings may be stretched across all of the columns which make up the story. This creates interest in the layout and avoids excessive white space to the right or left of a heading, depending upon its alignment, above a particular story. More information about headings is given in Chapter 9. If the column widths are narrow and a story with a long heading is to go

TAKE-OVER BID BY ALDERMAN FRUTINGER S.A. APPROVED

TAKE-OVER BID BY ALDERMAN FRUTINGER S.A. APPROVED

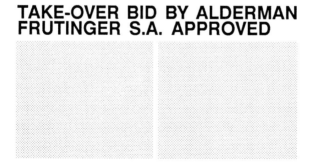

Figure 6.5   Accommodating a Long Heading

into one column only, you may choose either to halve the length of the column and so spread the story and heading across two shorter columns, or use a small typeface for the heading (as shown in Figure 6.5). The choice might depend upon both the layout's flexibility, and the importance of the story.

Apart from the adjustment of columns for headings, the same decision might be taken in order to incorporate an illustration without encroaching on other article space.

TEXT FITTING INTO COLUMNS

One of the special problems with column formats is fitting the text into the length of a column and ending articles at an appropriate point, so as not to leave uneven space at the foot of columns or to spread a story from one column to another with an awkwardly small amount of text.

Some desktop publishing systems provide what is called 'vertical justification'. This is an automatic facility which spreads the space between paragraphs of a block of text to the end of the given column depth. This is particularly useful if your story ends just a line short of the bottom of the column. You can spread the story to the foot of the column so that the bottom of each column is aligned across the page. This is achieved by the system calculating the amount of space left to fill the column and then dividing this space evenly between the paragraphs, so that only a small amount of extra space is added to each convenient break point. In this way, it may be difficult to detect that an extra space has been added.

Naturally, this works best only where the story runs slightly short of the column's depth. If the story was too short, the space placed between paragraphs would be excessive and the story would looked peculiarly spaced. When this occurs, it is perhaps best to find a way of using up the extra space, perhaps increasing the amount of space occupied by the story's heading, or by including a graphic at the end of the story as a space filler.

If the facility to justify text vertically does not exist on your system, and your story is, for example, one line short of the end of the column depth, then you can achieve a similar result manually by adding extra fractions of a line space between paragraphs, until you have used up the value of a full line depth. Whatever you do, try to spread the space evenly, rather than applying it to just one paragraph and always avoid changing the line spacing of the text within paragraphs to spread the text, as doing so will make the column look particularly untidy and is quite unprofessional.

7   Hyphenation and Justification

When producing various pieces of artwork on desktop publishing systems, the operator is often required to take decisions about making the best use of the space available on the page, as well as considering the æsthetic requirements of the job. When making decisions about these, the two factors which affect both space used and overall appearance are *hyphenation* and *justification*.

JUSTIFICATION

Justification of text is referred to in the phototypesetting sense of the word; that if text is *justified*, then it has both the left and right hand boundaries of the line width aligned (as the text in this paragraph, for example).

Some desktop publishing systems refer to different kinds of justification, ie left, right, centre and both-sides. Strictly speaking, while one might talk about text being left justified, the correct term is really range left or left aligned (or ragged right text). Similarly, text which is right justified should be called range right, or right aligned. The word justified is then reserved for text which is aligned at both margins of the column.

Justification in desktop publishing is achieved in the same way as it is for word processing, ie spaces between words are adjusted. As many words as possible are fitted onto a line without reducing the word spaces to such an extent that they are indistinguishable and then a new line is begun. The amount of space that is then spread between the words of the line will depend upon the length of the last word and whether words are allowed to be hyphenated. The space that would be occupied by a last word that would fit exactly is then divided between the number of word spaces on the line.

These lines are justified but the last word on the line is short, so the space between the words is not excessive.

However, in this case, by using a very long word like prestidigitation, without hyphenation, large word spaces result.

Figure 7.1   Word Spaces in Justified Text

Figure 7.1 illustrates how the word spacing is adjusted for the text according to the length and number of words on the line. When typesetting, this adjustment of word spacing takes place automatically and is not something which the operator necessarily controls. However, you can control what is called *spaceband* information. This is information about the minimum, preferred and maximum word spaces that are allowable, measured in points or fractions of a point. If you specify a minimum wordspace, then the justification will ensure that no word space is less than the minimum, and if necessary, carry a word at the end of the current line down to the next line. If the minimum were zero, then one could effectively continue adding words to a line until there were no word spaces at all before a new line is begun.

Spaceband information can also be used to specify appropriate letter spacing which may also be adjusted for justification purposes. For most practical purposes, however, the operator will find a suitable setting for these values and adhere to them, regardless of the type of work being set. If the minimum word spaces are not large enough, the text can easily appear cramped. If they are too large, then the word spacing can appear too open, and the text, particularly if set in a small typeface or with short line widths, can appear unnaturally spaced apart. The optimum settings should be arrived at by experimenting on different typefaces of varying sizes.

Choosing whether to use justification for aesthetic reasons is a matter of personal preference to a certain extent. However, you will probably find that, because range-left text means less hyphenation and more even word spacing, it may be best not to justify when the line length is short. Unjustified text is said to have a more relaxed look, with the varied line ending spaces allowing the type to 'breath', but this is a subjective point and should not be taken literally. Generally, justified text tends to have a more formal appearance about it and almost all books are set with justified type. Figure 7.2 shows text set in four different ways.

To be or not to be, that is the question. Whether 'tis nobler in the mind to suffer the slings and arrows of outrageous fortune, or to take arms against a sea of troubles, and by opposing, end them.

Range Left

To be or not to be, that is the question. Whether 'tis nobler in the mind to suffer the slings and arrows of outrageous fortune, or to take arms against a sea of troubles, and by opposing, end them.

Justified

To be or not to be, that is the question. Whether 'tis nobler in the mind to suffer the slings and arrows of outrageous fortune, or to take arms against a sea of troubles, and by opposing, end them.

Range Right

To be or not to be, that is the question. Whether 'tis nobler in the mind to suffer the slings and arrows of outrageous fortune, or to take arms against a sea of troubles, and by opposing, end them.

Centred

Figure 7.2   Text Layouts

The next part of this chapter concerns hyphenation which is closely related to justification. As shown in Figure 7.1 previously, unnecessarily large word spacing resulted when a word at the end of a line was too big to fit in the remaining space and so had to be carried down to the next line. By hyphenating the larger words which can be split into syllables, better, more even word spacing can be achieved in justified text.

HYPHENATION

In Figure 7.3, below, the examples are reproduced from Figure 7.1, but this time with an automatic hyphenation facility in place, provided by the desktop publishing software.

These lines are justified but the last word on the line is short, so the space between the words is not excessive, and there is no need to hyphenate any words.

However, in this case, by using a very long word like prestidigitation, but with hyphenation, word spaces remain reasonably consistent and of acceptable width.

Figure 7.3   Hyphenation Used on Justified Text

The difference in word spacing on the first line is indistinguishable from that in Figure 7.1, since there was no need to hyphenate any words. However, the second example has been improved considerably by hyphenation.

Hyphenation is a complex matter for typesetting systems to handle. In order to know which words can be hyphenated and at what point in a word a hyphen is acceptable, requires a considerable amount of information. Such information is supplied to the desktop publishing systems by *hyphenation dictionaries*. These are references for the software, which instruct when and where a word can be hyphenated. Even using such automatically controlled facilities, the decision about hyphenation made by a software package may be in conflict with your own opinion, or you may find, for example, that a word is hyphenated in an awkward place such as at the bottom of a right-hand page. So how do you control the hyphenation? Is it sometimes better not to use hyphenation? To answer these questions, you need to consider the following.

If text is *not* going to be set justified, then the use of hyphenation is likely to be reduced considerably. Whether hyphenation is used at all will depend upon how the word spacing looks and this will vary according to the typesize and the line length. Sometimes, a very slight reduction in typesize and a change in the spaceband information might be sufficient to prevent a word that would otherwise be hyphenated from being split. Apart from these measures, some desktop publishing systems provide a *discretionary hyphenation* facility. A discretionary hyphen is one that the operator chooses and is usually used to change the position of an automatically placed hyphen to suit an individual preference, or to take out a hyphen altogether. It may also be possible to switch off the hyphenation facility on an individual paragraph if there are too many hyphens causing the typesetter problems.

There are some guidelines about hyphenation which may be referred to when in doubt:

— do not hyphenate if there are fewer than two characters either side of the hyphen;

— do not hyphenate a number;

— do not hyphenate words of one syllable;

— avoid an excessive number of hyphens at the end of consecutive lines — two at the most;

— try not to hyphenate large headings or headlines.

If you are setting a narrow column of text, it is perhaps advisable to use a left-aligned format to reduce the amount of hyphenation that is necessary. Justified columns tend to suffer from over-hyphenation, and this can be irritating to the reader. When large headings are hyphenated, the word break often creates an impression of two separate words, far more so than in the body of a paragraph of text, and this problem is accentuated with larger typefaces and narrower column widths.

HYPHENATION DICTIONARIES

The hyphenation dictionary of a desktop publishing system is a catalogue of information used by the system to determine where a word should be hyphenated. You should not regard these dictionaries as the ultimate authority on hyphenation as there may be some cases where the placing of the hyphen does not always suit either the appearance of the line break, or the personal preference of the operator. In such cases you should override the hyphenation with a discretionary one, but do not manually hyphenate using the hyphen key, as this is regarded as a separate character, and will remain in the text even if the word position changes. Only use the hyphen key to indicate phrasal compounds (two or more words which are to be read together as a single word with its own meaning).

Different hyphenation dictionaries are required for different languages. Foreign languages have different sets of rules about how words are hyphenated, so make sure that if you set a publication in a foreign language you use the appropriate dictionary. Not all desktop publishing systems provide alternative dictionaries, but there are some available as supplementary software offerings from independent suppliers.

Hyphenation dictionaries vary from system to system. There is no definitive dictionary that is more of an authority than any other. Some desktop packages use a dictionary produced by specialists in the field of hyphenation, for example, PageMaker uses a 110,000-word dictionary, based on software by the Houghton Mifflin Company, called the 'Ranked Hyphenator System'. Above all, when using discretionary hyphens to override, or in place of, automatic hyphenation, try to be consistent throughout your publication, and write down your own set of 'rules'. This is particularly useful if other operators are to produce artwork and remain consistent with your own work. If you have more than one hyphenation dictionary, stick to using the one that you are most satisfied with, and do not mix them between publications.

HYPHENATION AND JUSTIFICATION CHOICES

The decision about when to hyphenate, and what sort of justification to use is largely a matter of preference and depends on the type of publication you are producing. When typesetting a book, manual, or similarly long document, it is popular practice to use justified text. Provided the typeface is not too large and the line length sufficient to allow a reasonable number of characters on the line, in most cases, the automatic hyphenation facility should be switched off. You would then use discretionary hyphens only where a line of text appears tight or cramped.

For newsletters and magazine-style publications, justified text may be preferable because it helps to define the boundaries of the column (see also Chapter 6 on multiple columns and column separators) and because the line length is generally short, automatic hyphenation will almost certainly be necessary to avoid excessive word spacing.

For special documents such as short reports, brochures, sales promotional leaflets, etc, the use of left-aligned text is commonly used. This is because the use of white space is considered to be more important in documents which require a shorter attention span. The text must appear more open and inviting, and left-aligned text has a natural tendency to suit these requirements. The text will also look less formal if unjustified.

The alignment of headings on documents and posters is a much more subjective matter. Right-aligned headings are best used in cases where there is only one column of text beneath. In multiple-column documents where more than one column carries a heading, it is generally better to use either left-aligned or centred headings. This is because the heading will be more clearly associated with the story to which it applies. Right-aligned headings in multiple-column documents may infringe visually on the space occupied by other stories, particularly if other headings use a different alignment. If right aligning a heading, always follow with either right-aligned text or justified text (see Figure 7.4). If you right align a heading but left justify the text, the two components will appear detached and the document will seem unbalanced (see Figure 7.5).

The
New Class
Curriculum

The development of this year's class curriculum has involved the Institute in the continued submission of strategy plans to the authorities. Maidwalk Educational Committee has presented a proposal, which was tabled in last week's general meeting, for our consideration. It was clear that the majority of attendees were satisfied that the proposal could be implemented without any significant delay, perhaps excepting articles 3 and 7 which require a slight restructuring in the administrative procedures in order to smooth the introduction of these new proposals.

Figure 7.4   Balanced Alignment

**The
New Class
Curriculum**

The development of this
year's class curriculum has
involved the Institute in
the continued submission
of strategy plans to the
authorities. Maidwalk
Educational Committee
has presented a proposal,
which was tabled in last
week's general meeting,
for our consideration. It
was clear that the majority
of attendees were satisfied
that the proposal could be
implemented without any
significant delay, perhaps
excepting articles 3 and 7
which require a slight restructuring in the administrative procedures in
order to smooth the
introduction of these new
proposals.

Figure 7.5   Unbalanced Alignment

8 Kerning and Character Compensation

The space between characters alters according to the shape of the character itself. For example, the capital letter 'A' has a slope on either side which means that the white space at the top of the character is greater than that at the bottom if you envisage the letter enclosed in a rectangle, see Figure 8.1, below.

Figure 8.1   An Example of Individual Letter Space

The space occupied by the character inside the imaginary rectangle determines the position in which the next character begins. If this next character has a sloping side also, such as the letter 'V', then there is additional white space at the bottom of the character which together with the space created by the 'A', appears to be more than the normal amount of character space. An example of this is shown in Figure 8.2, below.

Figure 8.2   An Example of the Illusion of Extra Space

The larger the characters, the more space there is between them and the more separated the characters appear to be. With combinations of certain letters like this the space between them can seem unnatural from an optical viewpoint. Other letter combinations, such as 'N' and 'I' do not have this problem since the sides of the characters are straight and no additional space appears between them when they are brought together. To compensate for this spacing problem, two special features of desktop publishing systems are employed: *kerning* and *character compensation*.

KERNING

By definition, kerning is the adjustment of space between individual letters so that one part of a letter extends over the character space of the other. Using the example mentioned earlier, and using rectangles to represent the character space occupied by the letters themselves, it is easy to see how the actual character spaces overlap to reduce the space between the letters. The apparent proximity of the letters in Figure 8.3 appears to be correct, and the letter fit and legibility is improved by the use of this technique.

Figure 8.3   An Example of Kerning

There are a number of letter-pairs which may be improved by the use of kerning. The common pairs are shown in Table 8.1 shown opposite. Desktop publishing systems often provide an automatic *pair-kerning* facility which recognises certain letter-pairs and automatically applies kerning to them. You may have to select this facility manually, or it may be built in without any option to switch it off. This process can slow down the composition of a page, however, so it is useful to be able to apply the kerning selectively, perhaps only on larger typefaces such as those used in headings. In fact, some systems will allow the operator to specify a minimum point size at which paired kerning will be automatically activated. This reserves the facility for selected typesizes only. Character kerning applies to both capital letters and certain pairs of upper and lower case letters, particularly where the upper case letter overhangs the lower case letter, such as in 'To' and 'Ye'.

AT	AY	AV	AW	Ay	Av	Aw
FA						
LT	LV	LW	LY	Ly		
PA	P.					
OV	OY					
RT	RV	RW	RY	Ry		
TA	Ta	Te	Tc	Ti	To	Tr
Ts	Tu	Tw	Ty	T.		
VA	Va	Ve	Vi	Vu	Vy	
WA	Wa	We	Wi	Wm	Wo	Wr
Wt	Wu	Wy	W.			
YA	Ya	Ye	Yi	Yo	Yp	Yq
Yu	Yv	Y.				

Table 8.1   Letter-pairs Needing Kerning

The term which relates to the method of producing the kerning effect is sometimes referred to as negative letter spacing. This is because the effect is actually achieved by changing the spacing between the letters by subtracting units of space from the adjoining letter. This mathematical operation is considerably easier than the traditional approach, in which the metal typesetter operator had to physically cut the two letter blocks to be kerned. Another form of kerning is one which is based on the shape of characters, this enables characters to be fitted together according to their shape, rather than by unit space reduction. This kind of kerning is called 'topographical kerning'.

Kerning is also affected by the typeface itself. Some typefaces have more pronounced spaces at the top or bottom of the character pairs than others. For example, in some typefaces the letter 'A' may have a vertical stroke on the right-hand side of the letter, rather than a slope. Therefore, you may notice the kerning effect increased or decreased according to the typeface that you choose. Not all character-pairs are kerned the same way in every typeface. Apart from the actual typeface, the size of the type determines how noticeable the kerning requirement is. As the typeface increases in size, so too does the space between the character-pairs that might require kerning. This is explained more fully in the following paragraphs.

CHARACTER COMPENSATION

As the characters change size, compensation for kerning has to be adjusted proportionately. If kerning is based on the value of the kerned increment which is usually specified as a percentage. Some specialised desktop publishing systems will allow you to adjust the percentage character compensation values so that the kerning for larger type sizes is tracked by the system to ensure optimum optical balance between kerned pairs. This system of tracking for kerning is referred to as *character compensation*. In those systems that do not provide any particular features to change the value of the compensation, this tracking will occur automatically, adjusting the kerned increment in phase with the typeface's point size. For example, a typeface of 24pt may have a kerned increment of 1pt, and a 12pt face may have half increments of 0.5pt.

Depending upon the type of screen resolution that you have on your desktop publishing system, you may find that the character compensation is not particularly apparent on screen. This is especially the case if the kerned increment is less than a pixel's width. However, if you are using a laser printer or phototypesetter as an output device, then you will probably find that the kerning is more pronounced on the printout than it is on the computer screen.

WHEN TO APPLY KERNING

In most cases, kerning will be activated by the system once you start using typesizes which are above 12pt. This is because 12pt is a popular typesize for the text in the body of a publication, and the requirement for kerning is less pronounced. Once you start using typesizes above 12pt, it is likely that you are setting headings or display type for posters, notices, overhead slides, etc, where the character pairs, previously shown in Table 8.1, will appear incorrect unless kerning is applied. You should get into the habit of being able to recognise when additional kerning is to be applied over any default values that the desktop publishing system may offer. It is surprising how many people do not notice the need for kerning until it is pointed out to them.

9 Headings and Opening Paragraphs

One of the areas of page design which catches the attention first and foremost is the heading and/or the opening paragraph. In typographical terms, a heading may be referred to as the display line. It is in this area that one can be much more creative, trying out a variety of possible typestyles and sizes, alignments and positions which one could not do with the body text of a document. Consequently, designing the heading of a publication can be quite fun. It can also be a disaster if not given enough careful thought. This is simply because display type is so outstanding, usually due to its size, that if chosen without care, it can stand out like a sore thumb.

The size of the heading can be important since it clearly portrays not only what the document is about, but also indicates the relative importance of the article, report or story to which it applies. Opening paragraphs can also be used to help emphasise the main point of a story, and may become decorative and inviting openings to a more lengthy document.

THE MAIN HEADING

The main heading is the one which is used to announce the nature of the publication. On a report, for example, the title of the report will be the main heading; on a book, the title of the book; on a magazine or bulletin, the name of the magazine or bulletin; on an overhead transparency, the name or description of the subject matter. As a main heading, it should carry more weight than all other headings in the publication. This means that it is generally larger, or perhaps simply in a bold typeface, or perhaps both.

The position of the main heading is important so that it stands out clearly. It must not conflict with other elements, such as a graphic or sub-heading which would detract from its importance, otherwise the impact will be lost. On the other hand, it should not dominate the page to such an extent that it unbalances the layout altogether. Figure 9.1, opposite, shows two examples of a page and heading. In the top part of the figure, the heading is rather too small. The sub-heading used in the document carries the same weight as the main heading, therefore it is not quite so obvious that the first heading is the main title, except that it appears first. In the example in the lower half of the figure, the heading has become more prominent, and is clearly not part of the text. A change in style and size means that the sub-heading is also more clearly defined.

One way of making headings more individual and clear is to use some of the features of desktop publishing for special effects. For example, you might try using a shaded background like this:

THE MAIN HEADING

Or perhaps an open text style often called 'outline' with shadows, like this:

THE MAIN HEADING

Figure 9.1 Main Heading Examples

By utilising these features, a main heading becomes more of a display type, and is clearly not part of the body of the text. Headings can also be separated from the rest of the document by using rules and graphics. The heading can be 'cut-off' from the body of the document, occupying an area of the page all of its own. This is particularly common in bulletins and newsletters, where the heading becomes a banner, but can also be used more subtly in a report-style document. Examples of these are shown in Figure 9.2, opposite.

Graphics, such as icons and line artwork associated with a heading should be used in proportion to the heading. If a graphic image dominates the heading, the heading will lose its impact. If the graphic is too small, it will look like an afterthought.

The position of a main heading depends on the kind of document and the alignment of the text below. If the document is a report with a single column of left-aligned text, it is usually better to left align or centre the heading. Right aligning of the heading can unbalance the page layout. If the text beneath is justified, any alignment may be satisfactory, but you will find that sans serif typefaces are more suited to right alignment than serif faces. This is because the serifs themselves can cause an optical misalignment at the right-hand edge, which is more noticeable, the larger the typeface and the more prominent the serif is in the type's design.

When a heading appears in its own banner area, the alignment of the heading is not so critical, but you should aim to keep the position and spacing of its components as evenly balanced as possible, otherwise the banner will appear like a 'window' of cuttings from newspapers.

Remember, when setting headings in large typesizes, to pay attention to letter spacing, ie the *kerning* of the type, to ensure that the special letter combinations are meshed together. For information about this, refer to Chapter 8 on kerning and character compensation. Also pay attention to the line spacing if the heading takes up more than one line. If a heading does have to be split over more than one line, make sure that you avoid hyphenation,

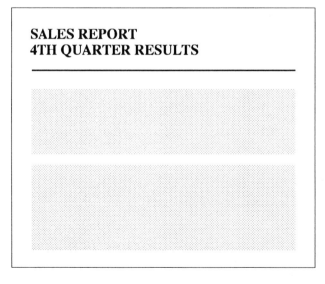

Figure 9.2   Heading Examples Separated from Body

and close up the line spacing so that the separate lines are brought together as a single block.

SUB-HEADINGS

Reports, manuals, brochures and other documents of length may often require sub-headings attached to paragraphs. The style and position of a sub-heading must not conflict with the main heading, so that there is confusion between the two. Generally speaking, the sub-headings are used at different levels. To distinguish one level of sub-heading from another, you can change the style, alignment, indentation or other attributes of the typeface.

For example, a paragraph heading at the first level in this book is in bold type and set in upper-case characters. The next level down, is also bold, but uses upper- and lower-case characters and so carries less emphasis. When deciding upon the amount of emphasis given to headings, you should work on a descending scale of styles which provide less and less emphasis, for example:

THE DEGREE OF EMPHASIS
THE DEGREE OF EMPHASIS
THE DEGREE OF EMPHASIS
The Degree of Emphasis
THE DEGREE OF EMPHASIS
THE DEGREE OF EMPHASIS
THE DEGREE OF EMPHASIS
The Degree of Emphasis
The degree of emphasis

Each of these examples carry a different degree of emphasis. Strictly speaking, with the facilities available in desktop publishing, it is not necessary (and indeed preferable not to) underline a heading which is already in bold. Underlining is used for emphasis on typewriters that do not have a facility for bold type, and, if using a courier typeface to mimic the output of a typewriter, underlining text, either as a heading or to emphasise points within a paragraph, is acceptable. Underlining may be used for aesthetic reasons, otherwise, most emphasising can be done by using bold or italics.

If you formulate a rule for the style associated with a level of heading, you will have to be careful to use the style consistently on all headings of the same level.

The amount of indentation applied to sub-headings can also be used to distinguish between the different levels, but you will need to consider the indentation of the paragraph text as well. Figure 9.3, overleaf, shows the use of different levels of sub-heading with various examples of indentation. Note that the text is always indented at the same level, or further in from the sub-heading.

The choice of indentation depends upon the width of the column, and indentation is not particularly well suited to narrow-column magazine-style work, where one does not generally indent text within a column width, except, perhaps, for lists or tables. On larger documents, such as reports and manuals, the use of indentation at heading levels can help to create a more interesting layout by adding some variety to the style of the page. This is especially useful in lengthy technical or reference documentation which can otherwise be cumbersome reading.

Sub-headings which are set back to the margin from the paragraph or body text are sometimes referred to in desktop publishing software as 'hanging indent headings'. Forcing a heading back into a left margin from an indent level, is sometimes achieved using negative indent.

USE OF COLOUR

Remember that colour may also be used for altering the character of display type and headings. If you are preparing artwork for litho print reproduction or have a colour printer which can be controlled by your desktop publishing software, think about the possibilities of adding variety and interest to headings by choosing a second colour. Should you be using a variety of colours, it may be that the styles you apply to various levels of headings are different from those that would be chosen if you were printing in one colour only. Bright colours give considerable emphasis to text, and the use of underlined or bold styles can then be kept to a minimum.

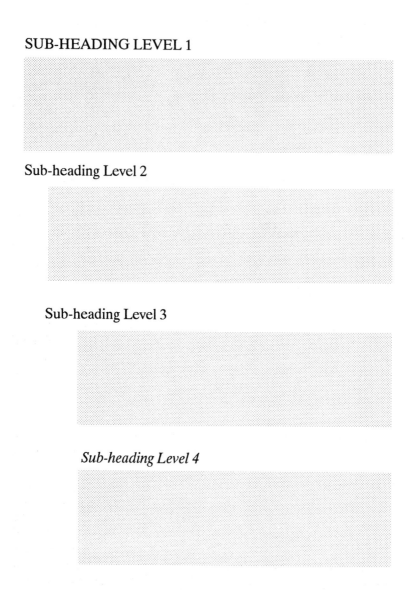

SUB-HEADING LEVEL 1

Sub-heading Level 2

Sub-heading Level 3

Sub-heading Level 4

Figure 9.3   Examples of Indented Sub-headings

OPENING PARAGRAPHS

In books, reports, newsletters, manuals, and other long documents, special emphasis may be given to the opening paragraph of the document or story. In newsletter-type publications, one often sees the first paragraph of a story set in bold type. This makes the introduction to the story stand out, and can be useful to draw attention to particular stories if used selectively. Perhaps the main story of a publication carries an opening paragraph in bold type or with a special, large initial capital letter (called a 'drop capital'), to make it carry more importance than other subsidiary stories.

Other ideas for opening paragraphs in newletters, magazines, etc include the use of a shaded area behind the text of the first paragraph, or even the use of reverse video text, though this may look a little heavy if printed in black and white. Some ideas are illustrated in Figure 9.4. In these examples, the purpose of a special opening paragraph is to draw attention to the story, and to single-out introductory text which may identify the content of the story in summary form.

More subtle ideas are required for other publications, such as books and reports. You rarely see books with bold or shaded opening paragraphs, because this style does not suit such publications. Instead, a favoured alternative might be an initial capital letter which occupies several line depths, or the setting of the first word in small capital letters, or a combination of both.

When using drop capitals, you should take care to use the correct alignment and spacing. Some desktop publishing systems automatically produce a drop capital at the appropriate position, simply by selecting this as a style attribute for a paragraph. If your desktop publishing system has this facility it will make life a lot easier, but you may find that it only works on certain typesizes, and leading selections unless you have a PostScript printing device. If you have to position a drop capital letter manually, then there are certain points that you should bear in mind about correct alignment. The top of the drop capital should be aligned with the ascender line of the first line of text, as shown overleaf.

The traveller will save both time and money by planning his tour carefully before leaving home. The handbook will help him to select the most interesting routes and the pleasantest resting places, and point out how each day may be disposed of to the best advantage, provided the weather is favourable.

The great majority of tourists visit Switzerland between the middle of July and the end of September; but to those who wish to see the scenery, the vegetation, and particularly the Alpine flowers in perfection, June is recommended as the most charming month in the year. For expeditions among the higher Alps the month of August is the best season; but above the height of 6500 feet snow storms may occur at any time except in thoroughly settled weather.

The traveller will save both time and money by planning his tour carefully before leaving home. The handbook will help him to select the most interesting routes and the pleasantest resting places, and point out how each day may be disposed of to the best advantage, provided the weather is favourable.

The great majority of tourists visit Switzerland between the middle of July and the end of September; but to those who wish to see the scenery, the vegetation, and particularly the Alpine flowers in perfection, June is recommended as the most charming month in the year. For expeditions among the higher Alps the month of August is the best season; but above the height of 6500 feet snow storms may occur at any time except in thoroughly settled weather.

The traveller will save both time and money by planning his tour carefully before leaving home. The handbook will help him to select the most interesting routes and the pleasantest resting places, and point out how each day may be disposed of to the best advantage, provided the weather is favourable.

The great majority of tourists visit Switzerland between the middle of July and the end of September; but to those who wish to see the scenery, the vegetation, and particularly the Alpine flowers in perfection, June is recommended as the most charming month in the year. For expeditions among the higher Alps the month of August is the best season; but above the height of 6500 feet snow storms may occur at any time except in thoroughly settled weather.

Figure 9.4   Examples of Opening Paragraphs

Now is the winter of our discontent made glorious summer by this sun of York; and all the clouds that lour'd upon our house in the deep bosom of the ocean buried. Now are our brows bound with victorious wreaths; our bruised arms hung up for monuments; our stern alarums changed to merry meetings, our dreadful marches to delightful measures.

Some examples of drop capitals show the initial letter taller than this, but it generally requires subtle choices of typeface and spacing to make this work. The left-hand edge of the drop capital should be visually aligned, especially where serif typefaces are concerned, otherwise the character might appear to be out of alignment with the text that follows, for example:

Now is the winter of our discontent made glorious summer by this sun of York; and all the clouds that lour'd upon our house in the deep bosom of the ocean buried. Now are our brows bound with victorious wreaths; our bruised arms hung up for monuments; our stern alarums changed to merry meetings, our dreadful marches to delightful measures.

Different characters require different optical alignment adjustments, according to the shape of the letter. Letters like 'C', 'O' and 'G' are typical examples. The bottom of the drop capital should align with the baseline of the text that comes immediately adjacent to the bottom of the character, otherwise the character will distort the appearance of the line spacing at this point.

Using small capitals with drop capitals is seen occasionally and is another way of adding style to the opening paragraph (see Figure 9.5). Small capitals are capital letters designed to match the x-height of the typeface and size of the paragraph text. Like initial

The traveller will save both time and money by planning his tour carefully before leaving home. The handbook will help him to select the most interesting routes and the pleasantest resting places, and point out how each day may be disposed of to the best advantage, provided the weather is favourable.

The great majority of tourists visit Switzerland between the middle of July and the end of September; but to those who wish to see the scenery, the vegetation, and particularly the Alpine flowers in perfection, June is recommended as the most charming month in the year. For expeditions among the higher Alps the month of August is the best season; but above the height of 6500 feet snow storms may occur at any time except in thoroughly settled weather.

THE TRAVELLER WILL SAVE BOTH TIME AND MONEY by planning his tour carefully before leaving home. The handbook will help him to select the most interesting routes and the pleasantest resting places, and point out how each day may be disposed of to the best advantage, provided the weather is favourable.

The great majority of tourists visit Switzerland between the middle of July and the end of September; but to those who wish to see the scenery, the vegetation, and particularly the Alpine flowers in perfection, June is recommended as the most charming month in the year. For expeditions among the higher Alps the month of August is the best season; but above the height of 6500 feet snow storms may occur at any time except in thoroughly settled weather.

Figure 9.5   Examples of Drop Capitals and Small Capitals

capitals, some desktop publishing systems provide 'small caps' as a style selection option. Otherwise you will have to use ordinary capitals, but choose a smaller type size. Although this is a matter of personal choice, the mixing of drop capitals and small capitals is not really advised, it is probably better to use one style or the other, rather than both.

10   Pagination

Pagination is the making-up of copy into pages, either by hand or electronically using the facilities of the desktop publishing system. In this chapter, a number of related topics are discussed, not just those concerned with publications that are multi-page documents. The process of copy-fitting is as relevant to the publication of a single-sheet flyer as it is to a book. Certain 'rules' on pagination are covered, and these are designed to help you improve the quality of a layout by making page breaks at points which do not upset the flow of the text.

PAGINATION PROCESS

If a publication is to form a multi-page document, then the carrying of text from one page to another must be done in such a way as to ensure that there are no awkward breaks in the copy. Sometimes, by nature of the typeface and spacing chosen, the amount of space on the page and the length of the copy make some page breaks at first seem unavoidably fixed. There are times, however, when it becomes necessary to change one or more of these controlling factors to improve the quality of the layout and to make a better page-break point.

For example, consider a case where the sub-heading for a paragraph falls at the foot of a page, while the text to which it relates, begins at the top of the following page. Clearly, the separation of the heading from its text is a bad page break, and some action must be taken to amend the situation. You will have to evaluate the spacing on the page to see whether, by removing some space or even editing text, you can make sufficient space to enable you to bring part of the separated text back under its heading. Alternatively, you may need to add space or copy on the page so that the heading itself is taken over to the following page so that it is reunited with its paragraph.

Another example is when a paragraph ends in such a way that you cannot fit the last word of the paragraph on the current page, and have to take it over to the following page, where it might be the only piece of text and, therefore, look quite detached. This situation is described in the section headed 'widows and orphans'.

PAGE ASSEMBLY

The process of pagination begins by assembling different components to make up a single page of artwork. These components may be blocks of text, lines of display type (headings, etc), boxes and rules, and line or half-tone illustrations. When these design elements have been combined in a balanced way to fit the given area for copy, the page is then said to have been paginated.

In many cases, desktop publishing systems provide the means to carry out this process electronically, using the computer's screen as if it were a paste-up table. However, this does not mean that the only way to achieve good pagination is by using the page make-up facility on the desktop publishing system. In fact, many users opt for a combination of page layout on the screen and manual paste-up of other components, such as illustrations. This is usually due to the fact that the time taken to process many different design elements, such as graphics and half-tones, on the screen is much greater than the time taken to process text alone. It is often quicker to produce a page layout of text items only, and add the graphics later. This situation will no doubt change as the technology and power of computer processing increases, making the mixture of complex elements less cumbersome to process. The ways of assembling pages, then, can be summarised as follows: pasting up the typeset text onto a paste-up board, together with graphic elements, to make a page; electronically pasting up all elements on the computer screen; or a combination of electronic and manual paste-up.

Widows and Orphans

These terms refer to loose items of text that get detached from the main body of the paragraph when the text is carried across a page break. The 'orphan', is the text that gets left behind on the bottom of a page, while the bulk of the text is carried over to a new page. For example, the first line or heading of a paragraph may occur right at the bottom of a page, while the bulk of the paragraph may be on the following page as shown in Figure 10.1.

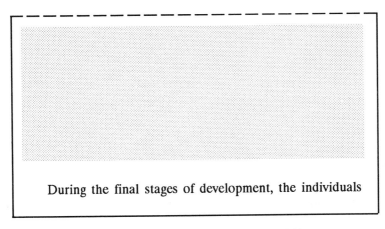

During the final stages of development, the individuals

Figure 10.1   Orphan on Bottom of Page

The 'widow' is the remaining text of a paragraph that gets carried over to the following page. The widow usually takes the form of a single word or perhaps one or part of a line of text. For example, if a paragraph does not quite fit into the space remaining, the last line of the paragraph, which may be no more than one word, has to be taken over to the following page. An example is shown in Figure 10.2.

It is generally considered that you should attempt to avoid these

at the end of the day.

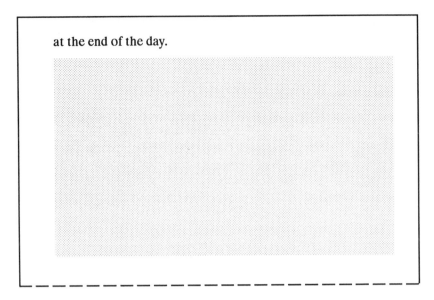

Figure 10.2   Widow at Top of Page

'bad' page breaks, though it is a matter of speculation how important this is. It becomes more noticeable in a book format, because there are so many full pages of text blocks. Certainly, leaving a heading behind as an orphan to the paragraph to which it relates is particularly bad practice, since the heading should always be closely associated with the paragraph (in terms of spacing, too).

HYPHENATED BREAKS

Another matter of subjective criticism of some publications is the practice of allowing text to be hyphenated from one page to another. If you look at examples of various publications, you will comes across those which do hyphenate from page to page, and those which do not. Generally speaking, it is perhaps best to watch out for hyphenated page breaks and see if they can be easily avoided, perhaps by using discretionary hyphenation to remove the automatic hyphen that may have been inserted, provided that this does not leave the line of text too spaced out or tightly packed.

If the two pages concerned are facing pages in a document, the problem may not be a serious one, since the eye can simply lead from one part of the word to another. However, if the hyphenation occurs at the bottom of, say, a right-hand page, then you will have to consider whether the hyphen occurs in such a position as to make the word unrecognisable in the first half of its hyphenated form. For example, if the page ended with a hyphenated word such as in 'the article was considered to be inappro-' one might clearly guess that the hyphenated word was 'inappropriate' and therefore not cause too much interruption in the flow of the text . However, if the following hyphenated example were to result: 'we wondered if the gentleman might be cont-' the hyphenated word could be a number of possiblities: 'content', 'contemptuous', 'contorted', 'contradictory', etc; the ambiguity remaining until the page was turned. The latter case may cause the reader to pause while deciphering the complete word in context.

TABLES AND LISTS

Tables and lists can be a pagination problem, and this problem is often encountered in reports, technical documentation and sales and product literature, where such things as lists of features, specifications and prices can be included at intervals throughout the document. These may unfortunately be positioned in such a way that the first four lines of an eight-line list of sales figures, for example, may be all that fits at the foot of the page.

Under these circumstances the action to take depends upon a number of factors. The design of the table of information can be one factor. For example, if a table is enclosed in rules and boxes, splitting the table between a page break may give the impression of there being two different tables. If the table includes important and relevant headings above a number of columns, then, by splitting these columns, the headings may need to be repeated, and, again, the effect of two separate tables becomes more apparent. If the table can include a broken line at the bottom which shows that it is continued, then this may help, but if the table contains figures which are best evaluated by being seen in one block (for example, to understand trends in a column of figures) then breaking the column can defeat the point of the table. Decide whether splitting the table disrupts its comprehension.

Another factor affecting the breaking of lists and tables across a page is the relevance of the position of the table or list in relation to the text. If the table can be referred to by a reference, and there is other text to follow, it may be best to insert a reference to the table at the relevant point, follow on with the text that would otherwise have come after the table, and position the table at the top of the following page, so that it is not broken by the page-break.

COPY FITTING

One aspect of a publication that may be useful to the desktop publishing operator is an understanding of how to fit copy into a given space on the page, according to the typeface chosen. Of, course, the electronic page make-up facilities help the operator to manipulate areas of text to fit into particular spaces, and by changing the typeface or typesize, column widths and margins, etc, one can usually make the text fit somehow. Suppose, however, that you are presented with the task of producing a company news-letter or brochure, for which someone else is going to provide the stories. As the editor of the job, you may be asked, 'how much do I have to write for the centre-spread article?'. You can either go by trial and error, or work to more carefully estimated word counts, if you know a little about copy fitting. Such information may also be useful, if you are presented with a disk of word-processed text for a manual and asked 'how many pages of typeset text will this make at A5?'. This latter question may be relevant if, for example, you want to get a quotation for the printing of a publication before you typeset the text itself and thereby find out how many pages it will make. There are two aspects of copy fitting that are useful indicators for fitting text, one is the character count, the other is the character per pica measurement of a given typeface.

Character Count

Each character in a document, including commas, spaces and

signs, as well as letters and numbers, needs to be counted so that you can estimate how much space the text will take up when it is typeset. For example, taking a manuscript that has been produced on a word processor, you may be able to find the number of characters on each line by finding out what the line width is, in columns, for the text file, ie if a column width of 60 has been used, then the characters per line could be taken as 60. The number of lines used per page in the text file may be shown, for example 60 lines, so one can quickly estimate an average of 3600 characters per page.

However, if you are presented with a printed-out copy with uneven line lengths, the task is a little more complicated. The best option under these circumstances is to draw a line down the right-hand side of the page to establish an average character count per line (see Figure 10.3).

There is a personality, an identity, about the various great
mountains, which only those who have long been intimate
with them can realise. No two are alike in configuration,
in height, in colouring; no two are similar in biography,
in history. Each, as has been well observed, has
"its physiognomy and character—its soul"—
yes, its soul. There is an actual personal equation
to be considered. The Jungfrau rose, afar off from the
bosom of the Lauterbrünnen Thal, holy and high and
pure, the bride of heaven, veiled and clothed in white
Fair is the valley of Lauterbrünnen, with its green
meadows and overhanging cliffs. The ruined castle
of Umspunner stands like an armed warder at the gate of the
enchanted land. In calm serenity the snowy
mountains rise beyond and from the topmost cliff, the white
pennon of the Brook of Dust shimmers and waves in
the Summer air.

Figure 10.3   Establishing an Average Line Length

Count the number of characters up to the drawn line, then count the number of lines on the page and multiply the two figures. If you need absolute accuracy, you should count every character. If you have access to the text as a word-processed file, you may have a facility within the software that will give you a character and word count automatically, which is by far the most accurate and simplest way to establish the character count.

If your word processor only gives you a word count, then, for general purposes, it is an accepted rule that words in English texts average five letters plus one space, so that the total number of characters divided by six gives a rough count of the number of words. Consequently, the number of words, multipled by six, gives a reasonable estimate of the total number of characters.

If you have a large document to work on, use two or three pages to establish an average character count per page, then multiply this average by the total number of pages in the document.

Characters per Pica

The next stage in the process is establishing the number of characters of a particular typeface that will fit into a one-pica space. For example, 10pt 'Helvetica' has a character per pica count of 2.5. Generally, the smaller the typeface, the larger the character per pica count value will be.

You can obtain tables of character per pica counts for various typefaces, either from the typeface suppliers, or from reference material on type. These tables will vary from typeface to typeface, and from one design of a given typeface to another.

You need to know what the character count is for different point sizes of the same typeface, and this is sometimes given as an 'alphabet length'. The alphabet length is the total length of a line of the alphabet set in lower case characters at a given point size. For example, take the following line of 11pt 'Dutch' (*'Times'* equivalent):

abcdefghijklmnopqrstuvwxyz

The length of this alphabet is 14 picas wide, which gives a character per pica value of 1.857.

Fitting the Copy

Having established the value for the point size of the typeface that the manuscript or copy is to be typeset in, the next thing you need to know is what the line length will be, in picas, for the typeset text (also called the measure). Assuming that the measure would be 32 picas, you can then detemine how many characters will fit on the line by multiplying the character per pica value by the line length — in our example, 32 x 1.857 which gives 59.42 characters per pica. This number now needs to be divided into the total number of characters in the original copy to obtain the total number of lines that the job will take. For example, if the copy was 28,000 characters, the job would result in setting 471 lines. This then is multiplied by the value of the leading to arrive at the depth of the setting in points. For example, if the leading is 12pts, the copy depth would be 5653 points. If the copy is mainly straight text, with no headings, then you can easily evaluate the number of pages that this setting will occupy, by working out the number of lines per page that will be set. Where headings and illustration spaces occur, these will have to be accounted for separately.

11 Illustrations — Captions and Referencing

Illustrations and pictures are worth a thousand words. A good line diagram can be useful in amplifying and clarifying main points in the text. Apart from its obvious benefit in this respect, the use of illustrative material in a publication, whether line illustration work or photographs, helps to break up the text which might otherwise seem monotonous (especially in a large document) and thereby retain the reader's interest.

Just how much illustration work to use will depend upon a number of factors, which include the facilities you have for producing illustrations, and how much costs are increased by their inclusion in the text. Scanner devices are very useful for including illustrative material which has already been produced in some other form, and the file generated by the scanner can be read directly into most desktop publishing software systems. Once stored on disk, the facilities in desktop publishing allow the pictures to be cropped, sized and positioned along with the text, so that they can be printed at the same time. Alternatively, you may find it easier to produce the illustrations separately and then paste them into place on the text artwork.

In some cases, the performance of desktop publishing systems is considerably hindered by the processing of graphics as well as text. This is because the desktop publishing software has to perform a great deal of screen processing, and as you change the screen contents, the software is continuously re-drawing the graphics as well as the text. The larger and more complex the graphics, the longer this process will take.

When you are carrying out text editing on a file that includes picture elements in it, the slowing down of the screen processing is quite noticeable compared to a text-only file. Some systems allow you to define the graphics input, then 'hide' the graphics until you choose to print the artwork, which helps in speeding up the screen processing.

Whatever method you use to include illustrative material in your document, you will need to carefully consider the positioning and size of the illustration, and how it is identified and referenced in the text of the publication. This chapter considers these factors giving some examples which you may like to follow, or use as a basis for your own ideas.

POSITIONING OF ILLUSTRATIONS

In some cases, the position of an illustration in a publication is dictated by the design of the page layout and the amount of text to be included. When paginating a publication (see Chapter 10), the fitting of an illustration at a particular location may be subject to the space left on the page at that point. The importance of the il-lustration is another factor, especially if there is only one illustra-tion to help identify the subject matter of the text which accompa-nies it. It may be helpful to the reader if the illustration appears either near the beginning or in front of the text, rather like the way a photograph in a newspaper is associated with the headline, rather than being slotted in somewhere else in the story.

Some documents are designed so that illustrations always ap-pear in a particular location. For example, in a technical manual, illustrations might be reserved for right-hand facing pages and always appear in the same position on the page so that a reader can easily see the illustration which accompanies the relevant passage of text. Alternatively, the illustration may appear directly below the paragraph that makes reference to it, or to which it is relevant. Some desktop publishing systems allow illustrations to be associated with a paragraph of text (sometimes referred to as 'anchored' illustrations). The space occupied by the illustation is linked to a particular paragraph, or perhaps a heading, so that, when the publication is edited, should this result in a change in position of the text, the illustration that is associated with it moves too. The position of the illustration is always dependent on the paragraph's own position, but difficulties may arise when the paragraph moves to a position where there is no room for the illustration, either above or below the text. When this occurs the text may need to be cut and pasted so that the illustration can be included.

The alternative to positioning an illustration so that it belongs to a particular piece of text, is to set it so that it remains fixed in position with relation to the page or paper. Thus, if, after editing, the text near the illustration moves, the illustration remains in the original position. In this case, you have to elect to either cause the text to flow around the illustration (otherwise text may overlap the illustration itself), or move the illustration to a new position manually. It all depends upon the facilities provided by your desktop publishing system. Some systems allow illustrations to be positioned on a page with text flowing round all sides (assuming there is the column width to do so), or so that it jumps over the illustration space and continues beneath. Examples of these positioning attributes are shown in Figure 11.1.

In multiple column page layouts, such as newsletters and magazines or brochures, illustrations may be positioned either within individual columns, or across several if the story itself continues over more than one column. It can be confusing to the reader if the illustration overlaps into other columns which belong to different stories, since a picture often acts as a pictorial heading in defining the boundaries of a story in a newspaper-style publication.

Another point about positioning relates to the way in which an illustration balances the page design. In a design which includes headings and text styles of various weights and sizes, the position and size of an illustration can affect the balance of the page layout itself. If the illustration is not positioned in harmony with the margins of the text or headings of a publication, it can throw out

The church keeps abreast of the times and has organ recitals every evening. The building dates from the sixteenth century — the towers are so old — but the foundation dates from AD 750, when a monastery of Benedictines was established here. This was the beginning of Lucerne. A small fishing village sprang up, which in 1291 was sold, with other Swiss fiefs, by the Abbot Berchtold to the house of Hapsburg.

This change of masters led to the formation of the league between the forest cantons, which Lucerne herself was slow to join. Indeed, her men attacked Unterwalden when the men of that canton were helping their confederates at Morgarten. In 1332, however, the town joined the league, and won a recognition of partial independence from her overlord.

a) Text jumps the illustration

The church keeps abreast of the times and has organ recitals every evening. The building dates from the sixteenth century — the towers are so old — but the foundation dates from AD 750, when a monastery of Benedictines was established here. This was the beginning of Lucerne. A small fishing village sprang up, which in 1291 was sold, with other Swiss fiefs, by the Abbot Berchtold to the house of Hapsburg.

This change led to the formation of the forest cantons, which Lucerne herself was slow to join. Indeed, her men attacked Unterwalden when the men of that canton were helping their confederates at Morgarten. In 1332, however, the town joined the league, and won a recognition of partial independence from her overlord.

b) Text flows around the illustration

Figure 11.1   Illustration and Text Positioning Options

A CASE FOR WILDLIFE

Preserving
our natural heritage
is now part of
everyday life.

More and more species need protection. It is in the interests of man, as well as beast, to ensure the future of our natural world. There are many plants and animals, some which no doubt remain undiscovered, that are invaluable to us. For example, plant extracts provide essential ingredients for drugs to combat disease.

The challenge to preserve nature begins in our everyday way of life. We should learn to consider the environmental consequences of the things we do and the things we use.

Text and picture elements above are not well balanced,
but below is a better arrangement.

A CASE FOR WILDLIFE

Preserving our natural heritage
is now part of everyday life.

More and more species need protection. It is in the interests of man, as well as beast, to ensure the future of our natural world. There are many plants and animals, some which no doubt remain undiscovered, that are invaluable to us. For example, plant extracts provide essential ingredients for drugs to combat disease.

The challenge to preserve nature begins in our everyday way of life. We should learn to consider the environmental consequences of the things we do and the things we use.

Figure 11.2   Balancing the Design Elements with Pictures

the alignment of the design elements of the page (see Figure 11.2 as an example).

In large format books and in some training texts, a large margin on one side of the paper is sometimes reserved for the illustrations. If you look at some examples of illustrated books, you may see those which include some full page illustrations, complemented by the use of smaller pictures alongside the text to which they are related.

If you do not position an illustration directly with the text, you will probably need to make some reference to it, and this is discussed next.

REFERENCING ILLUSTRATIONS

Whether you have to reference an illustration because it is not near the relevant text, or simply because it is part of your house style to do so, all text references to illustrations should be consistent throughout the publication. It is usually best to adopt some kind of convention about illustration references. For example, you may use figure numbers, like this book, where the figure number relates to both the chapter number and the number of the figure within the chapter. You may simply choose to refer to 'the following illustration' or the 'illustration opposite'. If you use figures, decide whether to refer to them as 'Figure x' or 'Fig. x' or 'fig x' etc, and stick to the chosen style throughout the publication.

Whether an in-text reference is required at all depends upon how you use illustrations. If an illustration is not referred to in the text (perhaps because it is simply for enhancing the presentation), the use of figure numbers is largely irrelevant. If the illustration is self-explanatory, or carries its own brief description, again, an in-text reference is unlikely to be required. Should you want several illustrations on a page with a single paragraph of text referring to them, you may either reference the separate pictures with 'a)', 'b)', 'c)', etc, or choose to identify the illustrations by their position on the page (such as 'top left', 'bottom right', etc). Again, whatever you choose, you should be consistent for each category.

In some texts, such as technical books or training documents, where many illustrations are used, it can be useful to make the in-text reference to the illustration stand out from the rest of the paragraph, perhaps using a bold typeface. This will help the reader find the relevant text for an illustration quickly. In such cases, the illustration is the key to the subject of interest to the reader. Other means that may be used, apart from bold text, are the use of italics or capital letters.

CAPTIONS

The caption on an illustration may be used for a number of reasons. For example, it may simply carry a figure number, so that the reader must refer to the text to find out more about the illus-tration. It may carry some title or brief description about the illus-trated subject as well as a reference, or may simply be a brief explanation of the illustration which excludes the need for any further explanation in the text.

The position of a caption may depend on whether it is also used as a heading, (in which case, it may be positioned above the illustration) or on how much text is around the illustration (you may be able to fit the caption alongside). It is usual to put a photo caption beneath the photograph, in a reasonably small typeface, perhaps italics. This is common for photographs of people, for example.

Figure 11.3 shows several examples of the use of captions with illustrations. As a guide to using captions properly, try to avoid using too large a typeface and do not use a typeface which is larger than the text size of the rest of the publication; unless there is a specific reason why the illustration should carry more importance than a paragraph or publication heading. Keep the space around a caption sufficiently tight so that it does not become optically detached from the illustration, and inadvertently appear to be part of the text. If an illustration includes text, such as a graph which carries its own axis headings, etc, use a typeface, style and size that does not conflict with the illustration's own text, as this may cause

Right:
The Great Seal

Johann Jakob Sulzer-Hirzel

FIG. 90.—Section of the synclinal on the Pilatus:

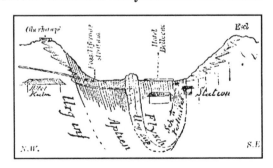

Figure 11.3   Illustration Captions

the caption to become lost in the illustration. For further ideas about captions, use styles that you find suitable from other printed material, but make sure you choose publications that are similar in purpose to the one you are illustrating.

12 Ruling and Forms Work

Most desktop publishing systems provide facilities for drawing lines and boxes. In traditional terminology, lines are generally referred to as 'rules'. Lines can be used to enhance the appearance of a page layout, and may separate components of a page, such as the heading, text area, running headers and footers, etc, from each other. In multiple column documents, vertical rules are used also in the column gutters to separate either columns or stories from one another. Boxes may be used as borders for banner-style headings, or even the entire page, eg when typesetting a certificate or notice. Illustrations may be bordered with boxes or separated by lines from the rest of the text.

Apart from the use of rules in page layouts to enhance appearance, rules are also used for producing forms work. In this area, desktop publishing systems generally have the edge over word processors, because they can provide both horizontal and vertical rules for building up a matrix or table. This chapter discusses the use of a desktop publishing system's drawing facilities, found in most page make-up software. (You do not need to have a drawing or graphics/paint software package for forms work, to produce a wide variety of forms for administrative use.)

Many internal forms are used in organisations, and desktop publishing systems provide an economical way of producing these as either artwork for photocopying, printing (printing will be necessary if multi-part forms are required), or by using a laser printer as the printing device to produce the number of copies required.

. LINE TYPES

Most desktop publishing page make-up software offers the user a choice of line thicknesses. The finest rule is generally the 'hairline rule', the next thickest a half point, then a 1pt, followed by successive lines in multiples of 1pt increments:

Hairline:

½pt Rule:

1pt Rule:

2pt Rule:

4pt Rule:

6pt Rule:

8pt Rule:

12pt Rule:

In addition to the straightforward rules, some systems provide a variety of special rules, useful for extra emphasis for boxes or borders, for example:

and 'coupon' rules, which are used for broken lines around coupons or tear-off slips, etc:

When using rules in a forms layout, the choice of thickness for the line depends upon a number of factors, for example:

— the thicker the box or line, the more important it is in the form layout, therefore, use different thicknesses for emphasis of particular boxes or areas;

— if the form is to be reproduced by some other printing method, make the difference between the thicknesses sufficient to enable the rules to be distinguished. Remember that thin lines may get thicker and thick lines thinner in the printing process, or vice versa;

— do not use too many different thicknesses of line in one form, otherwise the person completing the form will be confused about the priority or order of filling in;

— start by using the thinnest line that can be adequately reproduced without breaking up. Lines that are too heavy look like they have been drawn with a large marker pen, and produce an ugly form layout. Make the lines on the form appear less prominent than the weight of the typeface used for the text.

BOXES AND LINES

Boxes are used on forms to enclose a particular area of the page in which the form-fillers are to confine their input. A box defines the boundaries of the input area. When using boxes, therefore, consider the amount of information that is to be included, and the space that will be needed to enter the maximum probable input in the box. Consider, also, the way in which the form is likely to be completed. If the content of the form is going to be typed, it may not need as much space as hand-written details. Most handwriting occupies at least twice the amount of space as typed copy.

If a box is to take more than one line of input, consider whether you are going to add lines within the box to help the form-filler. For example, an address box may be broken up with lines. 'Empty' boxes tend to provide a more open and cleaner-looking form, than ones with lines. If you do decide to include lines inside a box, make sure that the thickness of the lines is less than the border, otherwise the box may look like several boxes, rather than one with lines inside.

Using lines alone produces a less official looking form, and tends to be ideal for coupons or tear-off slips. These type of forms generally require only a small amount of information. The more information required on a form, the more helpful it is to put things in boxes.

Lines should be provided where lists of input are required, as they help to establish the number of entries expected. Lines should also be used on forms that require answers to questions, since the inclusion of a line indicates that an entry is required, and that the text is not simply a description or heading.

If preparing an invoice or other business form that might be completed on a computer or typewriter, it is perhaps best to leave lines out of the area on the form where details will be printed or typed. Use a box instead, and vertical rules to separate the columns; including horizontal lines will only serve to make alignment of the form more difficult particularly when using a continuous-form printer.

Some examples of boxes and lines used in forms are shown in Figure 12.1. In order to find out which sort of rule work looks best for a particular form, try more than one version to start with, until you become experienced at judging the most appropriate style.

OTHER DESIGN IDEAS

Some forms require areas to be left uncompleted (perhaps those for 'office use') and others that are more important, compulsory, optional, or carrying some other peculiarity. Such areas on forms can be distinguished by using shaded backgrounds, particularly inside boxes. With some forms, boxes can be created by using an overall shaded background, leaving white areas of space where the

Layout No	Operation No	**OPERATION LAYOUT**		No
Drg No	Material	Batch Qty	Dept	M/C or group

No	Operation	Station	Travel	Cuts	Feed	R.P.M

Gauging procedure

Notes:

Detail	Gauge	Freq.

PERSONNEL: FACTORY AND OFFICE						
Age		18/30	31/40	41/50	60+	TOTAL
MALE	Factory					
	Office					
FEMALE	Factory					
	Office					

Figure 12.1   Boxes and Lines in Forms

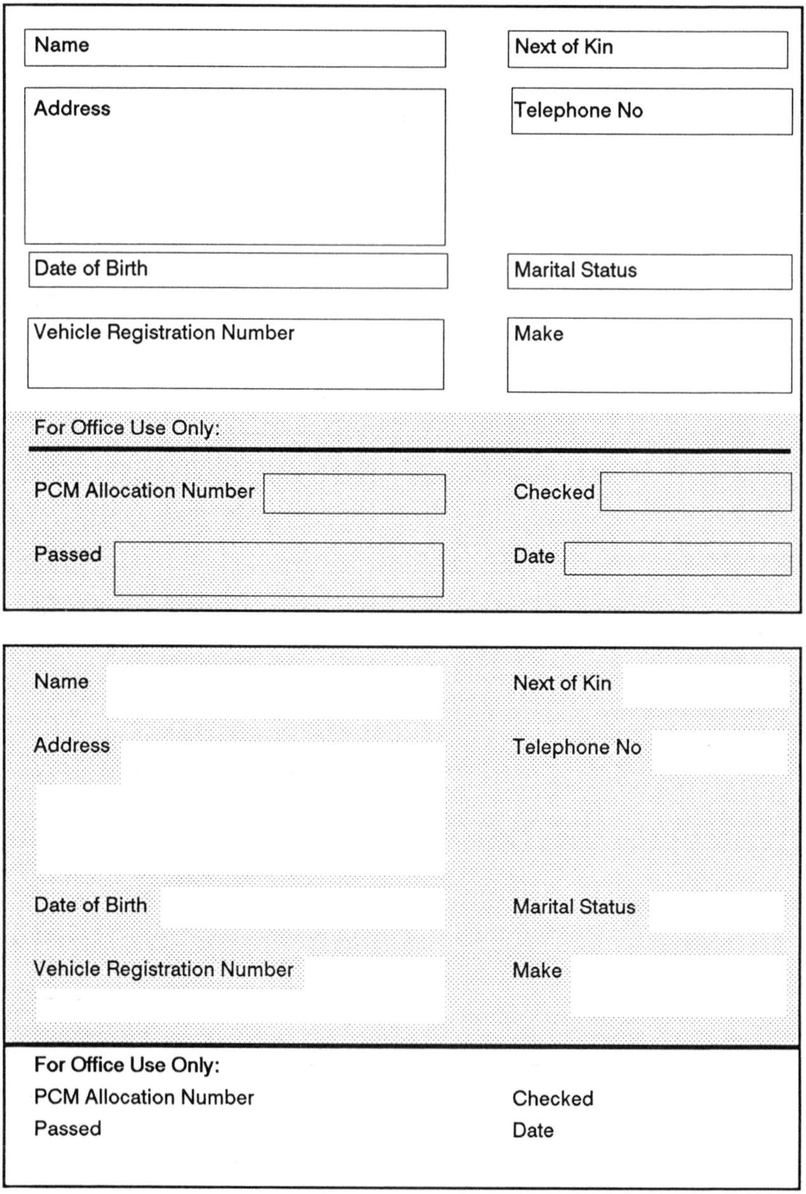

Name	Next of Kin
Address	Telephone No
Date of Birth	Marital Status
Vehicle Registration Number	Make

For Office Use Only:

| PCM Allocation Number | | Checked | |
| Passed | | Date | |

Name	Next of Kin
Address	Telephone No
Date of Birth	Marital Status
Vehicle Registration Number	Make

For Office Use Only:
PCM Allocation Number   Checked
Passed   Date

Figure 12.2   Forms with Shading

form is to be completed. Examples of these are shown in Figure 12.2.

PLACING TEXT AND HEADINGS

If you are using boxes on forms, you should always place the heading, instructions or title of the content of the box inside the area of the box itself, preferably in the top left-hand corner. The text should be easy to read and simple to comprehend. In many cases, a sans serif typeface provides a suitable style for forms, since it looks much clearer than a serif typeface when used for short phrases or single words.

Only place text or headings inside their own boundaries if there is a clear distinction between the content of the boxes, such as on an invoice or statement. If the reader of the form is going to receive a completed form (such as an invoice), then the contents will usually be distinguished from the headings by a different type quality and style (ie columns of information entered on a typewriter or dot matrix printer will stand out from typeset headings easily enough).

If the form is to be completed by hand, including the heading, questions or instructions in the box in which the reply is to be entered will help avoid confusion about how many boxes are to be filled in and which boxes should not be completed. Figure 12.3 shows how ambiguities can arise.

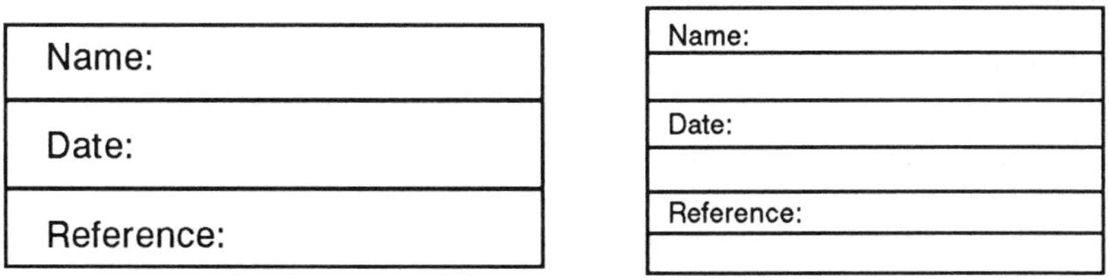

Good Style   Confusing Style

Figure 12.3   Avoiding Ambiguities in Headings

The headings should not be any larger or heavier than they need to be for the sake of clarity. Make sure that the balance between the weight of the rules is proportional to the weight of the text, otherwise the boxes on the form look ugly.

SPACING AND ALIGNMENT

Not all forms require a full A4 or other paper-sized area for the information. If the form is to be printed, you might choose a suitable design which, after printing, can be trimmed down to a manageable size, and adequately fulfil its purpose, while saving on reproduction costs. One can see examples of desktop publishing-produced order forms, questionnaires, etc, that have been produced on A4 which could easily have been completed on half or a third of the size of paper.

If the form is a business form for reproduction on continuous-form stationery, make sure that the spacing between lines of successive information is correctly set for the kind of printer or computer on which it will be used. Different computing systems have specialised spacing requirements, so make sure you check before designing the form.

If the amount of space is getting tight on a complex form, reduce the size of typeface for headings and the weight of the rules used for any lines or boxes. Always do this first before reducing the size of the boxes which are to be completed, and only when you have reached a reasonable minimum for these should you consider reducing the space given for input on the form. The person completing the form can then be assured of the maximum amount of space possible.

Keep the space around headings which are inside boxes even above and left, and make sure that headings are aligned, as far as possible, where boxes themselves align at the left-hand edge (see Figure 12.4).

Take care to ensure that all lines and boxes that can be aligned, are aligned. The form will look more professional if the alignment

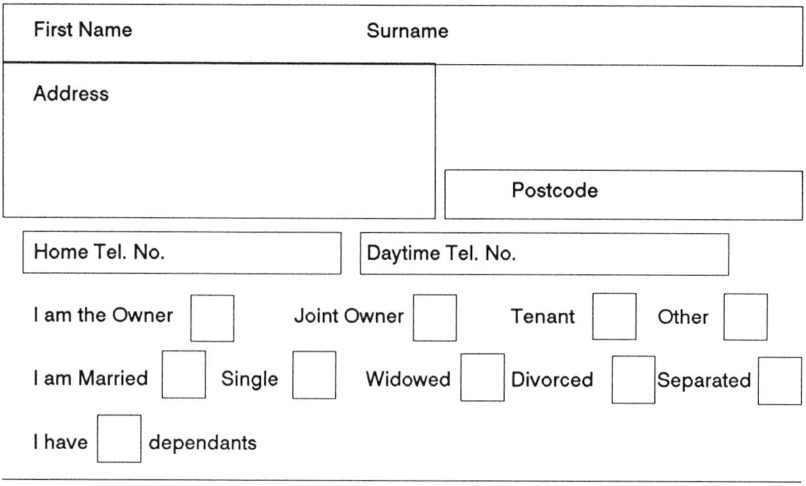

The above form has not been planned well, even though it may provide the necessary information. The same data can be rearranged with more care taken over the layout. The result should be a form which is easier to complete, as shown below.

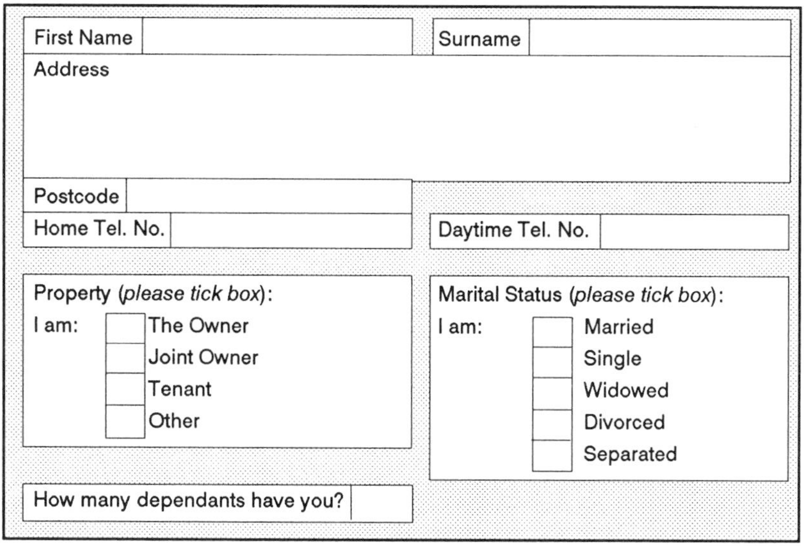

Figure 12.4   Alignment and Spacing Examples

of all verticals is accurate from left to right, across the form. This is more important than the horizontal alignment of the tops and bottoms of boundaries, since your eye is trained to look from left to right first.

13   Tables and Lists

Tables and lists are included in a publication as a means of presenting information which would otherwise be difficult to assimilate within a paragraph of continuous text, or not otherwise represented in some graphical way. Therefore, it is important that all lists and tables are clear and easy to read. Lists may separate words, numbers, phrases or even small paragraphs of description, which represent a series of distinct components within a publication. The manner in which tables and lists are typeset, using desktop publishing, can make the difference between the information being communicated both clearly and accurately and an otherwise ambiguous representation of the facts.

Tables and lists are discussed separately, although there is a certain degree of overlap in the points raised and advice is given for both. This chapter considers how best to use some of the facilities, of most desktop publishing systems, that can be called upon when you have to include a table or list in a publication.

TABLES

Tables, by nature, are made up of more than one column of information, and therefore the separation of these columns by an appropriate amount of space is important to ensure that they can be clearly distinguished. The alignment of the columns is also an imporant factor, so that lists which may include numbers and text of inconsistent lengths, can be brought together in a vertical alignment so that the column boundaries are not obscured; this requires the use of the tabular composition facilities available in most desktop publishing software.

Because tables are columnar, there is a tendency for desktop publishing users to make use of rules to separate the columns; perhaps even enclosing the columns of information in boxes. However, before you present the information in this way, consider whether the rules actually make the table clearer. If there are many rows and columns in the table, the table might end up with too many rules, and in such cases, clarity should be achieved by using extra space instead. It is arguable as to whether vertical and horizontal rules in tables make them easier to read, and the decision must be made on the content and purpose of the table. Horizontal rules may be necessary to separate sections within the table, though, again, in most cases, this can also be achieved with the use of additional space between certain lines of data.

Rules may cause the table to take up more space, than if they are omitted. The two tables in Figure 13.1 show how the same table of information can be set in completely different ways. In the first case, rules have been used to separate the columns of information. In the second table, the same information is set without rules, in such a way as to enable the information to be given in less space. Whether the first table is easier to read is a matter of opinion, but this example demonstrates that ruled tables can occupy more space. If you choose ruled tables, they should be set without being cramped, and without the lines being too close to the figures.

The other advantage of setting a table without rules comes from the fact that if the table requires modification, it may be easier to do so if rule lengths do not also have to be modified or repositioned. While vertical rules between columns has been criticised, rules may be used to separate column headings from the actual content of the table itself to good effect. If rules are being used in this way, then, as suggested in the chapter on forms work, you should choose the thickness of the line with care. Do no use more than one or two thicknesses in a table, unless there is an important

Production, Sales, Foreign Trade

Situation with regard to orders, production, sales and stocks in industry (Index 1975 = 100)	1984	1985	1986	1987	1988
Incoming orders	149	158	160	165	177
foreign orders	156	169	169	166	184
domestic orders	147	152	154	160	171
Orders in hand	124	130	133	126	127
Industrial output (1963 = 100)	151	159	165	166	178
Sales	133	142	147	149	159
Stock of finished products	118	123	129	134	130
Change compared to previous year in %					
Incoming orders	11	6	1	3	8
foreign orders	25	8	0	-2	11
domestic orders	4	3	1	4	7
Orders in hand	8	5	2	-5	1
Industrial output	3	5	4	1	7
Sales	6	7	4	1	7
Stock of finished products	4	4	5	4	-3

Production, Sales, Foreign Trade

Situation with regard to orders, production, sales and stocks in industry (Index 1975 = 100)	1984	1985	1986	1987	1988
Incoming orders	149	158	160	165	177
foreign orders	156	169	169	166	184
domestic orders	147	152	154	160	171
Orders in hand	124	130	133	126	127
Industrial output (1963 = 100) ..	151	159	165	166	178
Sales	133	142	147	149	159
Stock of finished products	118	123	129	134	130
Change compared to previous year in %					
Incoming orders	11	6	1	3	8
foreign orders	25	8	0	-2	11
domestic orders	4	3	1	4	7
Orders in hand	8	5	2	-5	1
Industrial output	3	5	4	1	7
Sales	6	7	4	1	7
Stock of finished products	4	4	5	4	-3

Swiss Federal Statistical Office, Berne, Switzerland

Figure 13.1   Two Versions of a Table

disctinction between them. A thicker rule will indicate that the information associated with it may be of greater significance. Where a distinction has to be made in this way, make sure that the thickness of the line is sufficient to be noticeable after printing, since thin lines can come out thinner and thick lines can come out thicker in the printing process, and vice versa.

If a table is particularly long, it is a good idea to improve the ease of reading by inserting a space after every five or six lines. Tables often have a 'landscape' format to them, and you need to decide whether or not to set the table sideways; then the reader must turn the page to see the table. Since turning the page for some tables and not others may be a nuisance, you should try to avoid setting sideways. In most cases, you should find it possible, by dividing or re-designing the table, to set it on a normal portrait-page orientation.

Choosing what size of typeface to use in a table will depend on the space you have available for it. In a publication that has more than one table, the size of typeface will be determined by the largest table, ie the largest one that will fit on the chosen page layout. You should try to avoid making the typesize too small, so that the table becomes difficult to read. Once a size has been defined, use the same size for all tables in the same publication. Important items in a table can be highlighted in bold, but you should choose a bold type which can easily be distinguished from the roman version. Some serif faces, for example, are not obviously distinguishable in bold from their roman face, and sans serifs are usually better when mixed in bold and light weights.

Placing tables in multiple-column documents can cause problems at times. If you include a table in a newspaper or magazine style layout, you should avoid placing the table in the middle of the page, since it can interfere with the reading continuity. If the table cannot be fitted into a single column width, allow ample white space around it, and, if possible, include it at the top or bottom of the page, so that it is clearly separated from the rest of the page layout. Columns of figures should have vertically aligned columns in order to remain clearly readable, and avoid ambiguity. The desktop publishing system is likely to offer a variety of tabular composition facilities, including various means of aligning both text and figures against a particular tab stop. Keep your tabs evenly spaced and when you are setting in a proportional typeface, use the *decimal alignment* facility to ensure that figures align either side of the decimal point. Tables 13.1 and 13.2 show the difference between setting with and without decimal alignment.

Column 1	Column 2
12.34	42.67
132.45	142.56
43.0	253.12
1092.32	312.55

Table 13.1   Setting Without Decimal Alignment

Column 1	Column 2
12.34	42.67
132.45	142.56
43.0	253.12
1092.32	312.55

Table 13.2   Setting With Decimal Alignment

Table 13.3 illustrates how decimal alignment can align even those lists of figures which are set inconsistently (some have trailing decimal places, others do not). For the sake of clarity, however, it is best to use decimal alignment, showing fractional amounts thus:

Column 1	Column 2
12.34	42.67
132.45	142.56
43.00	253.12
1092.32	312.55
112.30	1115.00

Table 13.3   Setting Showing Fractional Amounts

National Income
Per Canton

Canton 1987	Million Sfr.	Percentage of total CH = 100.0	Sfr. per inhabitant	Position*
Zurich	48,766	21.6	42,676	4
Berne	28,431	12.6	30,440	12
Lucerne	8,499	3.8	27,372	21
Uri	890	0.4	26,331	23
Schwyz	3,018	1.3	28,688	17
Obwalden	722	0.3	25,512	26
Nidwalden	1,000	0.4	31,546	10
Glarus	1,494	0.7	40,161	5
Zug	4,705	2.1	56,550	1
Fribourg	5,760	2.6	29,165	15
Solothurn	6,655	2.9	30,113	13
Basel-City	10,051	4.5	51,623	2
Basel-Country	7,719	3.4	33,945	6
Schaffhausen	2,241	1.0	31,832	9
Appenzell A. Rh.	1,373	0.6	27,405	20

*according to income per inhabitant

Swiss timber production and consumption
(in 1000 m³ round timber equivalent)

	1981/5	1986	1987
Domestic Consumption	4,190	4,628	4,570
Imports	4,810	5,782	5,861
rough timber	442	492	362
waste wood	376	386	393
semi-finished products	2,768	3,341	3,375
paper and cardboard	1,223	1,563	1,731
Exports	2,327	2,812	3,147
rough timber	697	668	800
waste wood	15	22	14
semi-finished products	704	907	1,004
paper and cardboard	911	1,215	1,329
Calculated total timber consumption	6,673	7,598	7,284

Swiss Federal Statistical Office, Berne, Switzerland

Figure 13.2   Sample Tables

Two further examples of tables are set in Figure 13.2. These show the use of spacing between figures and bold type to distinguish particular items.

LISTS

Showing lists of information within text is in some way related to tabular work, in that a list should be clearly set out with adequate space between the lines or paragraphs, so the reader can distinguish one item from another. You would not use rules in a list as they would force the list into being a table. A list is often indented, so that it is clearly distinguished from the rest of the text. The amount of indentation is arbitrary, but it should be reasonably balanced, so that any space to the right of the list is no less than that on the left. If there is no indent on the right of the list, then the amount of left indent should not be too large, otherwise the list will appear to be right aligned. If the lines or items in the list are short, you may consider centring the list, though for uneven line lengths, centring can make the list more difficult to read, unless you add extra line spacing between the items. For example, the second version of the following list is clearer.

Designed for comfort
Manufactured to British Standards
High-quality components used
Guaranteed for five years
Real value for money

Designed for comfort

Manufactured to British Standards

High-quality components used

Guaranteed for five years

Real value for money

The longer the list, the more important it is to space the items. Centred lists are only really suitable for items which occupy no more than one line. If the list is of a series of statements or more descriptive information, it is better to left align the list, and distinguish the items by the use of an em dash or bullet. For example:

— do not place the unit close to a source of heat, or in direct sunlight;

— keep the unit in a dry atmosphere. Excessive humidity will cause the unit to be easily distorted;

— allow at least 12 inches of space between the back of the unit and a wall, so that the air intake filter has room to operate;

— when the unit is not in use, disconnect from the mains and replace the safety cover.

The above list can be further improved by ensuring that the second or subsequent lines of text are aligned with the first character in the first line of each paragraph. The example below shows the same list with the better alignment of indented text, and with a bullet, used to highlight the start of each point being made:

- do not place the unit close to a source of heat, or in direct sunlight;

- keep the unit in a dry atmosphere. Excessive humidity will cause the unit to be easily distorted;

- allow at least 12 inches of space between the back of the unit and a wall, so that the air intake filter has room to operate;

- when the unit is not in use, disconnect from the mains and replace the safety cover.

This second example looks much more clear and precise than the first, and the use of the bullet as opposed to the em dash gives the points more emphasis, therefore they appear more important. As with tables, whatever method of presenting lists you choose, you should be consistent throughout the same publication.

14   Page Control

GENERAL

This chapter on page control covers aspects of the choice of page format and size, and the use of headers and footers, with numbering, in respect of a multiple-page publication. Selecting the format for the page depends upon the purpose of the publication. Most laser printers are capable of handling A4 copier paper as a standard size, and the tendency is for nearly all publications to be composed to this format. However, you should try experimenting with other sizes, particularly if the publication does not necessarily warrant the use of an A4 page. Most desktop publishing systems offer various page sizes as standard within A4, and some provide tabloid and A3 formats which can be printed as 'tiled' sections, each up to A4 which butt together to make up the full-sized publication.

You will need to consider the way in which the publication is to be reproduced. If a laser printer is being used as the printing device for the job, then the size of the job will be dictated by the capabilities of the printer. If litho printing is being considered, using the desktop publishing system as the artwork production device, then a whole range of possibilities exist for size and format.

Most desktop publishing systems offer printing in either lanscape or portrait format. For reports and letters, portrait will always be the choice because most business communication is in this format. A landscape format may be chosen for an illustration, table or presentation aid, where the design does not permit the use of a portrait format. Landscape formats might be considered when printing an A5 publication which will be folded from an A4 sheet. Using this facility, it is possible to print a four-sided publication on a standard A4 sheet without the need for any special finishing or stapling.

If the publication is of several pages, you will probably be using some form of page numbering, and perhaps even a running header to identify the publication on subsequent sheets. In these cases, the size and orientation of the publication will affect your choice of header and footer style; this is considered next.

HEADERS AND FOOTERS

Headers and footers are lines of information printed at the top and bottom of the page, respectively. They are usually used for identification of the publication, page numbering, dating and similar uses. In books and technical documentation, running headers may be used to identify the chapter or section, so that the reader always knows in what chapter a certain piece of information can be found or is being read. Page numbers may be included as part of either a header or footer, and may carry other information, like a volume, chapter or section number as well.

The amount of space assigned to a header and footer should be in proportion to the main text area of the page. In other words, the header or footer carries supplementary information only, and should not, therefore, be any larger than necessary to convey the information required. The emphasis should be on the main part of the page which carries the message of the publication.

Some technical and training documentation is produced with very large header and footer areas, and the distinction between a chapter heading and the running header is not always easy to determine in these cases. Sometimes, the header and/or footer area is separated from the main text area by the use of horizontal rules, but these should not be so heavy as to detract from the important information contained in the main body of the

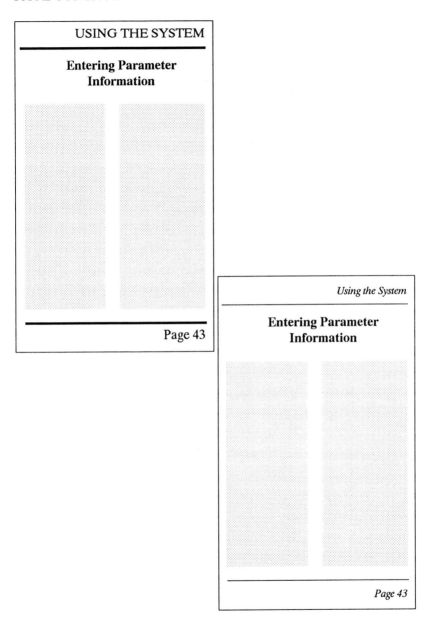

Figure 14.1   Examples of Header and Footer Areas

document. Figure 14.1 opposite illustrates this problem together with a more appropriate alternative. The factors which should be considered with regard to headers and footers include the following:

— the information to be included;

— the typeface to be used: should it be different from the main text or not?;

— the size of typeface: generally it is smaller than the main body, unless there is sufficient separation by space or rule from the text area;

— the alignment of the header and footer: this may change for left- and right-hand pages in publications that are double-sided and have facing pages;

— the amount of space between the header and the first line of text or the last line of text and the footer;

— whether the header or footer area warrants any rules or boxes;

— the style of page numbering to be used, if included.

Each of these will be considered in turn in the paragraphs that follow.

Content of Header/Footer

The header or footer is generally used to convey supplementary information which may assist the reader in locating information within a document or identifying the current section of a publication. This can be achieved by using one or more of a combination of items:

— name of publication;

— name or number of chapter or section;

— page number;

— date of publication;

— document reference;

— product name;

— filing reference or folio;

— name of author/publisher;

— name of recipient.

This is only a small sample of possible pieces of information that may be included, but you should only use the minimum amount of information for the purpose. If you fill a header or footer with too much information, it will become cramped.

Choice of Typeface

Whether the typeface you choose is the same or different from the rest of the text in the document is up to you. Often running headers in books (this book being an exception) are typeset in an italic or generally smaller typeface than the main body of text. Another alternative is the use of all capital letters in the same typeface (such as this book). Both methods are used to distinguish the header from the rest of the type.

Changing to a different typeface is sometimes used in formal documents and technical material, but it serves no typographical purpose other than to make a heading stand out from the other text.

The Typesize

If you use the same typeface and style as the main text of the document, you should perhaps consider using a smaller typesize for headers. The page number, however, need not be made smaller unless there is footer or header text alongside, in which case it should be in the same size as the rest of the header or footer. As a general rule, it is best not to set the header or footer text in a typesize larger than the main document text, otherwise it may be mistaken for a sub heading.

Alignment

In this book, the alignment of the components of the headers varies from the left- to the right-hand page. The page number is always on the outside of the page so that, when flicking through the book, the reader can always locate the page number easily. If this were not done and the page number on a right-hand page was close to the centre of the binding, the reader would have to open the pages more fully.

For running headers or footers which exclude page numbers, the alignment may be centred for consistency or, if it is simple enough to do with the facilities in your desktop publishing software, may change from right to left alignment according to whether the page is a right- or left-hand facing page.

Spacing

You should always leave sufficient space between the text area and a header or footer to separate it clearly from the text. This is even more important where rules are not used. A full line space might be sufficient if the header typestyle and size is easily distinguished from the text, but otherwise more space may be needed, as illustrated in Figure 14.2

The space between the header and footer and the top and bottom of the paper, respectively, should be no less than the space between the header or footer and the text area, otherwise the page layout will appear cramped.

Where there is no footer, pages which end at different points from the bottom of the paper can appear untidy, and may be improved optically by using a hairline or line rule along the bottom

Swiss Life in Town and Country

through the gradual evolution of the centuries, worked out a political constitution which is in its way quite unique. Although the world has seen, and has still before its eyes, other experiments in democratic government, there is nothing in existence, or to be found in the records of history, at all like what we see in Switzerland. Moreover, the interesting point is − to Englishmen, at least − that the Swiss constitution, like that of Great Britain, has been one of slow and step-by-step growth. Beginning, so to speak, in a single germ, it has, by a method analogous to that witnessed in other organised bodies, gradually developed new powers and differentiated functions, in accordance with the demands of the time and . . .

Swiss Life in Town and Country

through the gradual evolution of the centuries, worked out a political constitution which is in its way quite unique. Although the world has seen, and has still before its eyes, other experiments in democratic government, there is nothing in existence, or to be found in the records of history, at all like what we see in Switzerland. Moreover, the interesting point is − to Englishmen, at least − that the Swiss constitution, like that of Great Britain, has been one of slow and step-by-step growth. Beginning, so to speak, in a single germ, it has, by a method analogous to that witnessed in other organised bodies, gradually developed new powers and differentiated . . .

Figure 14.2   Headers, Footers and Spacing

of the page which draws the eye down to the same position on each page and gives the impression that the page is more complete.

Using Rules and Boxes

When using rules and/or boxes in headers and footers, make sure that they are not too heavy. A box tends to be more dominating than a ruled off header or footer, and is a gimmick sometimes seen on training manuals or technical publications. For documents such as reports, books, brochures and booklets, boxes are best avoided, unless there is a particular use for them.

The width of rules should be the same as the column width of the main text area, and headings that are right or left aligned should therefore align with the end of the rule. Space the rule from the header or footer enough to make the header or footer text readable, but make the space between the rule and the main text area larger, so that the rule is clearly associated as part of the header or footer area, and not 'floating' on the page.

Page Number Styles

There are various ways in which page numbers may be displayed including the following:

— arabic numerals, eg 1, 2, 3, etc;

— arabic numerals and the word 'page', eg *Page 2*;

— all-text page numbers, eg *Page four*;

— roman numerals, eg I, II, IV, or i, ii, ix, etc;

— page and section number combinations, eg 2-4, 3-12, etc.

The style chosen depends upon the type and size of the publication. The use of all-text page numbering is usually only reserved for brochures and leaflets with few pages. Books are nearly always set with arabic numerals only. Roman numerals may be used for small publications, but are usually reserved for the title pages of a publication or the appendices, with arabic numerals being used for the main section of the publication. All-text page numbering may look flowery, but is not suitable for large publications where the page number forms part of a referencing system or index.

15 Suiting The Style To The Job

One of the most important aspects of design and that which requires most experience, is suiting the design of a publication to the purpose for which it is intended. It is not surprising that, with graphic artists and typographical designers being employed by advertising agencies and printing studios for professional publishing, the skills required are not likely to be easily come by for the novice desktop publishing system operator. Yet, the very fact that desktop publishing within the computer industry has put the tools for publishing and print design into the hands of the layperson, means that the user of this new technology is encouraged to take on the role of designer and typesetter, especially for any publications which can be printed internally.

The result is that the type of design work that would have previously been undertaken by a skilled designer is now being attempted by the layperson using the facilities of desktop publishing. In order to avoid the many pitfalls in this skilled area, the operator, or the individual responsible for in-house publication, should ensure that the experience and knowledge required to achieve good results is nurtured among the staff whose task it is to produce the artwork.

To help in this respect, there are many organisations who are willing and able to train individuals in design and layout principles, and every opportunity should be taken to use these training facilities to compensate for the absence of sufficient experience, background knowledge or readily available expertise. Where you are providing artwork for particular printing jobs, it is a good idea to consult your printer's representative for advice about the most appropriate form of design for a particular job. Your ideas may be easy to realise on a desktop publishing system, but may have various economical consequences when put to the print process. You will be unable to predetermine these without a good working knowledge of the basics of print and design.

The simplest rule of thumb is not to run before you can walk. Start by producing the simpler and less important publications. The decision to leave the design of any publication which is used to reflect the image or status of an organisation in the hands of the novice must be carefully considered. Designing logos, headed stationery, brochures, and sales promotional material requires professional skills to achieve optimum effect, and unless the desktop publishing user takes the time and trouble to acquaint him or herself with good basic design skills, there is a risk that a poor quality layout will harm the company's reputation.

Ambiguities are a frequent problem with poor designs. An unfortunate use of typestyles, alignment and spacing can cause a communication to send the wrong message to the reader. The reason, therefore, that suiting the design to the job is such an important issue is highlighted by the increasing criticism of the quality of output from desktop publishing systems; criticism especially from the professional designers. This chapter cannot possibly hope to provide the necessary information to teach these skills, as the material involved would be sufficient to fill several books. Instead, the intention is to start the reader thinking about suiting designs to particular jobs, and it is then for the individual to seek further guidance and acquire experience in order to make the best use of the facilities provided by any desktop publishing system.

This chapter, then, is the first rung on a fairly long ladder of design skills and offers simple guidance on a few specific publication type jobs, not all of which will apply to the reader, which will serve as a series of examples of design considerations associated with specific printing and publishing applications. Apart from reading books on the subject, the student of typography and design can learn a great deal by being inquisitive and critical about the different types of publishing material that one encounters in everyday life.

STATIONERY AND LETTERHEADS

Many users of desktop publishing systems produce letters which incorporate a letterhead, or just stationery for use on typewriters or word processors. The task appears to be a simple one at first, but, because a letterhead may carry an organisation's image, it is one which is in fact quite difficult to achieve successfully; particularly where a logo has to be produced as part of the stationery design process.

The positioning of the elements of a letterhead requires careful consideration. The components of the information may include name, address, telephone number, telex number, fax number, registration number, name of directors, etc. The size of paper used is also important for the right selection of typeface and size. When laying out ideas for letterhead stationery, always view the various samples you produce in their completed form. Since a letterhead is supposed to be presented with a letter typed on the paper, view your samples by typing a letter as well, so that you can see how the position of the elements in the stationery balance or complement the layout and type of the body of a letter.

Many letters are typed with a margin, and it is useful, therefore, to make any left or right aligned text on a letterhead meet the margin that would otherwise be reached by the typewriter or word processor. Each margin should be even all the way down the side of the page. The left-hand margin may need to be larger than the right-hand edge to allow for filing and binding of the actual letter or a copy of it.

The style of the letterhead should convey the image of the individual or company it represents. If the organisation is modern or 'high tech', a clean, sans serif typeface might be suitable. A legal practice or consultancy, private bank, etc, might require a formal

UNIVERSITY OF LONDON

DEPARTMENT OF BUSINESS STUDIES

CLAREMONT STREET, LONDON
TELEPHONE: 071 234 5678

smith and jones advertising

54 saint john's mews
london
sw1

telephone: 071 234 5678
fax: 071 345 6789

Howard, Barnes and White
Solicitors

Medway House
Causeway Road
Hendon
Middlesex

Telephone: 081 987 6543

Figure 15.1   Examples of Stationery Designs

style using a more sombre approach with perhaps a serif text. Some examples of stationery are shown in Figure 15.1.

The colour used on stationery, if the artwork is for litho printing, can affect the intensity of the text. The company name on a letterhead might stand out more in a bright colour than it does in the black and white artwork proof, and an address, perhaps in a lighter shade, may well appear more subdued when printed. These factors can only be taken into account by looking at other examples of printing in similar shades, and with experience of which colours can be matched to good effect, so that the right components of the letterhead are given emphasis. If the stationery is to fit particular envelope sizes, window envelopes or other special stationery, this may affect the position of the items in the letterhead. If the stationery is to be used on more than one paper size, such as 'with compliments' slips, business cards, etc, the design must be suitable to work on all such correspondence material, not just the A4 letterhead.

There are no real rules about the layout of letterheads other than ensuring that the result is tasteful and practical. It is always good practice to try several designs, and if you are using your desktop publishing system to produce artwork for clients, it is important that you submit a number of possibilities with a wide range of typestyles and positioning alternatives.

The typestyle and size should, above all, match the words. Company and other organisation names are usually fairly short, so the choice of letter style is more important than would be required for a long document. The letters in the name must work well together in the chosen typeface, and remember to apply kerning to large typesizes to avoid the impression of uneven letter spacing. For formality, all capitals is usually better than upper and lower case letters combined. If using upper and lower, or all lower case characters, using a bold and weighty typeface gives the impression of a more substantial organisation than a lightweight typeface. But this is all a matter of taste for the designer, and when producing work for clients, what the client thinks is more important at the end of the day.

GENERAL STATIONERY

As previously mentioned in Chapter 12, forms work is another popular use for desktop publishing systems. A great many of the forms that are used internally by an organisation can be adequately prepared using the facilities of a desktop publishing system. The design of forms should be clear, and unambiguous. Choose a design that suits the purpose and the individuals who will be using it. Make provision on the left of the page for filing, so that punched holes can be put into the form without obscuring the content of the form itself. Make instructions and questions on forms clear, and use rules that are of an appropriate weight for the emphasis that needs to be given to a particular area, and no heavier than necessary. If a form is to be completed on a printer or typewriter, space the lines and rules so that they can be completed using the normal pitch and vertical spacing of the printing device for which they are intended (for example, six lines per vertical inch is commonly used for computer printers, with a character pitch of 10 characters per inch horizontally).

Address labels can be produced on desktop publishing systems using special A4 sheets of self-adhesive labels suitable for photocopier or laser printer use. When producing a label that includes your own address, make sure that the address is not so dominant that the post office might become confused about which address is the addressee, especially if the recipient's address is also produced on a laser printer or word processor using a similar typestyle. Some organisations may wish to frank addressed labels before thay are stuck onto envelopes, in which case, the address should be located at the foot of the label.

Envelopes can be processed by many laser printers, and you may wish to indulge in printing your logo or name on an envelope. The same rules apply to envelopes as to address lables. Avoid ambiguity about which address is which, and leave room for postage stamps and any other labels which may be required. There is a whole range of envelope sizes, and it may be quite economical to design an address or logo that can be printed onto a variety of envelopes, which will provide a smart presentation at a lower price than conventional overprinting. Remember that some papers are better suited to the laser printing process than others, and may therefore take the toner in different ways. Do not be tempted to put envelopes through laser printers if adhesive is likely to come into contact with the rollers of the printer as these get very hot and can be quickly messed up by melted gum. Some examples of other stationery designs are shown in Figure 15.2 overleaf.

PRICELISTS, TIMETABLES, ETC

Many publications are intended to be used for what are called 'information graphics' and these include such publications as technical documentation, specifications, wallcharts, timetables, pricelists, guide books, instruction cards, etc.

In each case, the job of the designer is to assemble the components of the publication in a lucid and logical order. The layout of technical information is particularly important to avoid ambiguities. Timetables, on which the reader relies for an accurate representation of the facts, and from which an absolute ability to obtain a given piece of information is essential, must be designed with care. Spacing and column headings are used for clarity of the information, and any special symbols used should be clearly explained.

Pricelists, too, must be clear, particularly if a matrix of prices applies for different markets. If you produce a typeset pricelist on your desktop publishing system, make sure you can understand which price applies to any given item or market. Do the prices include discounts or tax, and is this clear to the reader? Test out your designs on individuals in your organisation.

Like business and private stationery, make sure that the design and style used for information publications is suited to the readership. The style used for a theatre programme may be 'classical' in appearance if the play is a Shakespeare, for example, but may require a more modern approach for a Pinter production. When presenting directories and lists, such as internal telephone directories, make sure that your tabular design is spaced in such a way

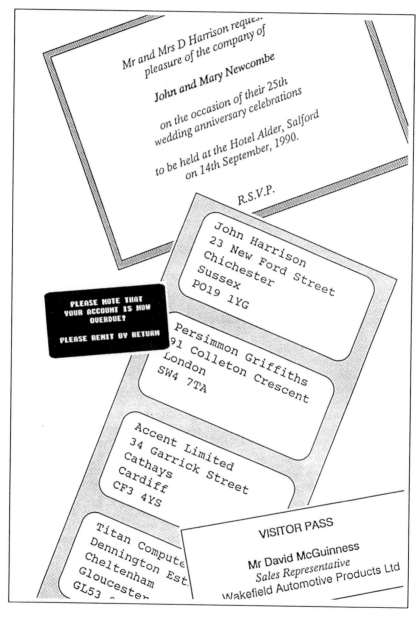

Figure 15.2   Sundry Design Examples

that enables a corresponding number to be easily associated with the name. Using leader dots, for example, can help align a number or price with an item, if the distance between the two columns is relatively large. If too much white space is put between columns of figures in lists and timetables, the reader may easily read-off the wrong value, time, etc.

16   Print Production

Many desktop publishing systems are used to produce artwork which is then taken to a printer for reproduction. This may be done because the print number is too high for the capabilities of the laser printer, or simply to utilise the facilities of a quality print process to present a publication of a more complex format, such as a 16-page brochure, book, colour leaflet, etc. In a book on design for desktop publishing, it is relevant to discuss print production (together with print finishing), for two reasons. First, any individual looking to improve their skills in typography and design can benefit from understanding the background of the printing process itself. Some of the features of desktop publishing systems may be specifically employed for print reproduction, such as the inclusion of crop marks when printing a page, or the ability to produce separate sets of artwork for colour separation. Secondly, if a publication is going to be printed using modern print technology, the process of print production may be relevant to the design considerations. For example, the choice of a particular page layout, typeface, graphic or scanned photograph, may be influenced by the quality of the paper, the print finish (covered in the following chapter) and the use of colour, etc.

One example of the latter consideration is that the use of colour in printing allows for alternative ways of emphasising text. Whereas in a single-colour publication, you may choose to use bold or italic typefaces to emphasise headings or items of interest and importance, the use of another colour may achieve the same result. Consequently, this will affect the use of typestyles within the publication itself. Learning about print production can be useful when trying to understand how page planning (called imposition) affects the number of pages you include in a particular publication (particularly, long documents and brochures) and how this may affect the ultimate price of a print job. The page size you choose may also affect the price, especially if you select an unusual size, which cannot make the best use of the print area available on a standard paper size or print sheet.

The next section provides a background of the lithographic print process, which is the one most likely to be encountered. The origination of type in other processes, such as letterpress will not be relevant to desktop publishing users, and is therefore excluded from this chapter. Another print process — Gravure — is an expensive, high-quality, high-print run process which the author believes is unlikely to be used by the desktop publishing user, therefore this is also omitted. Should you wish to find out more about the other print processes, there are many books available in bookshops and libraries which will be of benefit in this respect. Indeed, you may wish to investigate in more detail the litho print process after picking up some brief details in this chapter.

Your local printers will also be a useful source for guidance as far as artwork is concerned, and you should get into the habit of consulting them for assistance before producing artwork on your desktop publishing system. They may be able to offer some helpful advice which may result in making the process of transferring artwork to plate that much easier and probably cheaper too. Some printers are also willing to show clients (or indeed potential clients) around their premises, and this may provide invaluable practical experience of how the printing process is performed.

When you have decided on the best way to reproduce a publication from your desktop publishing system, spend some time evaluating how the design of the publication can be tailored to suit the characteristics of the process and finish that will be used. A design that clearly has not had the advantage of careful consideration and attention to detail and which is to be reproduced using a litho print process, can easily look ten times worse when it is printed than it did in artwork form.

LITHOGRAPHIC PRINTING

This method of printing is also known as offset or offset-litho and is the most widely used method of printing. The basis of lithography was pioneered by Aloois Senefelder in 1798. He used a flat stone onto which an image was applied with a greasy material and the surface was then wetted. Greasy ink was added next and this was absorbed by the greasy parts on the surface, but repelled by the wet parts. Prints were taken from the surface by laying paper over the stone and pressing. The paper would then pick up the image from the inked areas.

In offset lithography, thin flexible metal plates, which are wrapped around a cylinder, replace the flat stone. By being wrapped around cylinders, the process becomes suitable for rotary presses which enable long print runs at high speed, by being fed with paper from a roll (known as the web-fed process). The plates themselves are cheap enough to produce to make lithography a suitable printing method for nearly all types of printing.

The term 'offset' which refers to nearly all lithographic printing processes, comes from the fact that the image on the metal plate is offset (printed) onto a rubber blanket which is wrapped around a rotating cylinder. The image is then transferred from the blanket to the paper. In other words, the paper does not come into direct contact with the metal plate. This is important because it prevents the plate from become damaged by the rough surface of the paper, and because less water comes into contact with the paper from the blanket than it would if the image was transferred directly from the lithographic plate. Another advantage of the process being offset is that rubber is a flexible and malleable material. It can respond to the unevenness of the paper's surface, moulding itself to the contours of the paper, which would not be possible with a metal plate. Consequently, the image reproduction is clearer on more irregular surfaces, enabling litho printing to be suitable for a wide range of papers and materials.

IMPOSITION

Having produced page artwork, a printer will need to orientate the pages in such a way so that, for each side of a printed sheet, the correct order will be achieved once the sheets are folded and cut. It is this process which often influences the choice of the number of pages that are included in a publication, since the effective use of the printed sheet area can affect the cost of a print job. It is for this reason, for example, that a brochure might be more economically printed if eight pages are used, rather than seven or nine.

If a print job is to be produced as an eight-page document, then the imposition of the pages might be like this:

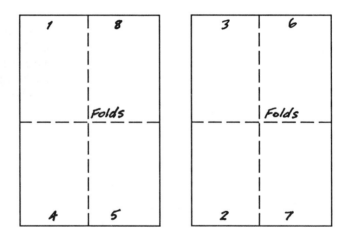

This would produce an eight-page job like this:

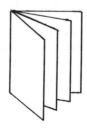

Alternatively, the imposition could be altered so that the page orientation appears like this:

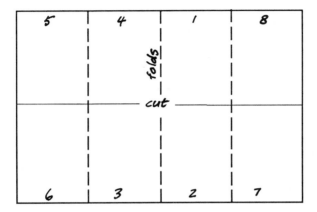

Producing an eight-page job looking like this:

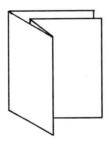

Paper is an expensive part of the printing process, so careful planning is important to make the best use of it. When printing brochures, books and long documents, the following fomula might be useful. To work out the number of sheets of paper that are needed to print a brochure or book (excluding the cover):

$$\frac{\text{No of books} \times \text{No of pages in book}}{\text{No of double-sided pages}} = \text{No of sheets required}$$

To work out what number of copies can be produced from a given quantity of paper, use the following formula.

$$\frac{\text{No of sheets} \times \text{No of double-sided pages}}{\text{No of pages in book}} = \text{No of copies}$$

The size of the page when trimmed (actually referred to as the trimmed page size) will determine what kind of printing machines and finishing will be used on the print job, and, therefore, the cost. A small print job produced on a simple press will be cheaper than if produced on a complex, fast press, since the set-up time will be in proportion to the scale of the task. This should be kept in mind whenever you are searching for a printer for a particular print job. For example, if you use your desktop publishing system to produce artwork for a letterhead which is to be printed in two colours, there is little point taking it to a multi-colour litho press. While they may be able to produce the letterhead, the cost, particularly if the print run (quantity) is low, will be too high. It is better to take it to a smaller outfit who has a two-colour press, or even a single-colour press which can take the paper through in two passes using different coloured inks each time. It all depends upon your requirements, and the skill in print buying is to match the task to the appropriate printing service to get the best results and value for money at the same time.

Using Table 16.1 as a guide, according to the number of pages in the publication, you can see what the maximum trimmed page sizes would be from a press size sheet measuring 1100 x 1600mm.

If you want to maximise on the use of a press, then you should select page sizes which are closest to the maximum for the number of pages required. If you have doubts, discuss with your printer what the optimum values are for their particular machines. Apart from the page size and use of colour, the cost is particularly dependent on the print run (the quantity of copies). This also affects the kind of printing machine a job will be produced on.

When assessing the quantity that you want printed, it is always

No of Pages	Maximum page size (mm)
8	538 x 394
12	522 x 269
16	392 x 269
20	309 x 266
24	266 x 261
32	195 x 266
48	193 x 178
64	193 x 133

Table 16.1   Maximum Page Sizes from Print Sheet

worth asking the printer to quote you the *run-on rate*. This is the cost for an extra number of copies for the same job, if printed at the same time, and is usually given as an average number of pages. For example, the cost for printing 1000 copies with a run-on rate of the cost for an extra 100, 200 or 500 copies. In most cases, the run-on unit cost of a job will be considerably less than for the initial quantity quoted. This is because, while the press is set-up and paper is available, the cost of running off 100 or so extra copies will be largely a material one. It might be worth having the extra copies printed if you think they can be used, which will be cheaper than getting a reprint later.

TYPES OF PAPER TO USE

There is a vast range of paper qualities available for various types of printing jobs, and the choice of paper depends on the type of print job, the effect you want, the cost of the job and the suitability of the paper to the print process being selected. Some of the more widely used classes of paper are described in the following paragraphs.

Newsprint

This type of paper is made from ground wood pulp and not

surprisingly is used in the printing of newspapers. It usually has a rough side to it, so the reproduction quality varies, and it is not suitable for detailed reproduction. Most newsprints discolour easily when exposed to sunlight for any length of time.

Wood-free

Paper described as wood-free is not, actually, free of wood. It is still chemically made from wood pulp, so if you are thinking that you might be being environmentally friendly by using this type of paper, you are wrong. Wood-free paper is strong, carries a good whiteness, and is suitable for a wide range of uses, from stationery to magazines. Bond paper, typically used for letterheads, is wood-free paper.

Cartridge

Cartridge papers were originally used for making cartridges. They are strong, but not very white. White cartridge has been bleached and is used for drawing paper. Offset cartridge is perfectly even-sided and is used for quality offset printing.

Featherweight Antique

Used mainly for books, it is thick and 'fluffy', and can make books look thicker than they would otherwise appear. It is currently used by only a few printers. Because of its rough surface, it is not well suited to half tones or line work with fine detail.

Art paper

Art papers are coated papers. They are usually coated with china clay and calendered (a smooth finish produced by passing paper through polished steel rolls of varying temperatures and pressures) to give a high quality gloss surface. They are particularly suited to high quality, fine detail work and can easily cope with the reproduction of half tones and colours; they are used extensively for glossy magazines. Other types of art paper include the matt art paper which is also coated with china clay, but not given the high polish of art papers in general. The surface is still very smooth, however, and therefore suitable for high quality reproduction. Apart from the art papers which are machine coated, there are 'imitation' art papers which are produced by adding a mineral loading to the wood pulp, and then they are highly calendered. Imitation art papers are quite good for reproduction of half tones and line work, but do not have the high quality of the machine coated papers.

17   Print Finishing

How a publication is going to be finished and presented may affect the design and layout characteristics. A report that is going to be comb-bound, or ring-bound, for example, may require a layout that provides extra space in the left-hand margin, to avoid holes being punched through the text.

The finish of documents is even more important when litho printing is being used. In the publication of a book or manual, where both sides of the paper are printed on, the gutter between the two pages needs to be greater at the centre fold than at the outside margins of the page. Many desktop publishing systems will produce this facing and double-sided page effect for you by selecting the option as part of the page layout attributes. If this extra space is not provided, then when the book is bound, the text near the centre of the page will be more difficult to see, and this problem is accentuated by the process of perfect binding (see description later), in which the book's pages do not lie flat as easily as they would if comb- or ring-bound.

The finish of a publication may also dictate the paper size used. Some processes are cheaper if standard sizes are used for binding equipment and accessories. For example, ring binders are available in standard sizes for A5 and A4, whereas other sizes may have to be assembled specially to order. While this is not in itself a problem, the economics of the print job have to be considered too. Obviously, any system of binding which deviates from standard facilities and practices is going to be more expensive as a result. As a guide to standard paper sizes, the following table has been included for reference purposes:

Size	Inches			Millimetres		
A0	33.11	x	46.81	841	x	1189
A1	23.39	x	33.11	594	x	841
A2	16.54	x	23.39	420	x	594
A3	11.69	x	16.54	297	x	420
A4	8.27	x	11.69	210	x	297
A5	5.83	x	8.27	148	x	210
A6	4.13	x	5.83	105	x	148
A7	2.91	x	4.13	74	x	105
A8	2.05	x	2.91	52	x	74
A9	1.46	x	2.05	37	x	52
A10	1.02	x	1.46	26	x	37

Table 17.1   'A' Series Paper Sizes

This system for sizing paper was established in Germany in 1922 and is sometimes referred to as DIN A size. Each size is arrived at by halving the size immediately above it, so it is simple for scaling purposes, since they all have the same geometric shape.

The 'A' paper sizes always refer to the trimmed sheet size, untrimmed sizes are referred to as RA or SRA. Another series of paper sizes used for those in between the various 'A' sizes is the 'B' series, but this is relatively uncommon.

Apart from standard paper sizes, it is useful to known the standard book sizes for book and manual print finishing purposes. These are shown for the United Kingdom (UK) in Table 17.2 and the United States (US) in Table 17.3 respectively. Note that the UK book sizes show the names of the various formats which might be referred to by a printer.

millimetres	inches
140 x 216	5.500 x 8.500
127 x 187	5.000 x 7.375
140 x 210	5.500 x 8.250
156 x 235	6.125 x 9.250
136 x 203	5.375 x 8.000
143 x 213	5.625 x 8.375

Table 17.2   Standard US Book Sizes

Quarto		
name	millimetres	inches
Crown	246 x 189	9.69 x 7.44
Large Crown	258 x 201	10.16 x 7.91
Demy	276 x 219	10.87 x 8.62
Royal	312 x 237	12.28 x 9.33
Octavo		
name	millimetres	inches
Crown	186 x 123	7.32 x 4.84
Large Crown	198 x 129	7.80 x 5.08
Demy	216 x 138	8.50 x 5.43
Royal	234 x 156	9.21 x 6.14

Table 17.3   Standard UK Book Sizes

There are a whole range of papers used for printing or publishing, some of which were described in Chapter 16. If you are printing from your desktop publishing artwork, the paper used must suit the printing process and you should consider the appearance and weight. The weight of the paper is important if you are going to send printed material by post, since a heavy paper can add considerable cost to the mailing bill, especially if the quantity is large, for example in a mailshot. This same consideration should be taken into account when laser printing mailshot letters. While heavier papers have a higher-quality feel about them, and have less of a 'show through' problem (most apparent on double-sided printing), it can be costly to mail.

The weight of paper is generally measured in gsm or g/m^2 (grams per square metre). This is the weight in grams of a sheet of paper one square metre in size. Paper may also be referred to in pounds (lb) weight.

Laser printer paper now commonly available for use with desktop publishing systems is a high-white paper of 100 or 115 gsm weight, while normal photocopying paper is 80 gsm. Most laser printers print more successfully on papers that have a fairly rough surface on which the toner can key. Exceptionally smooth papers or art papers tend to cause the toner to smudge during the printing process.

TRIMMING AND BINDING

As already mentioned, the method of binding to suit the publication and budget of the job may affect the style and design of the artwork required. There are various ways of binding documents and books, which range as much in price as they do in quality. Convenience is another factor to be considered when choosing the appropriate binding. For example, in a document that may require constant updating, a ring-bound method may be the most suitable. Any method of binding which cannot be updated without destroying the existing binding may be very inconvenient for technical and financial information, which is subject to change on a regular or ad-hoc basis.

Convenience may be important if you are going to carry out the binding and finishing processes yourself. If you are producing a document at A5 size from laser printer A4 paper sheets, you will have to trim the paper to size. To help with this, many desktop publishing systems allow you to print crop marks on the paper, where the size of the printed page is less than that of the paper size used in the cassette of the printer. Even then, trimming many sheets to size can be cumbersome without the right trimming equipment and many desktop publishing systems print the page in the middle of the paper. For example, an A5 sheet with crop marks is almost always automatically centred on the paper, meaning that the trimming must be done on four sides. An alternative might be to print two A5 sized pages, side by side on A4 paper, so that it can be cut in half to make the A5 sheets — one of the advantages of the 'A' series paper sizes. The printed sheets are collated and folded and trimmed to give the appropriate finished paper size. (Most printed sheets are trimmed after folding.)

Your trimming requirements may vary according to the method of binding adopted. If the paper is to be folded and stitched, the pages will need to be trimmed after folding, otherwise the edges of the paper will be misaligned, especially if there are many pages in the publication. You may need to consider leaving larger gutters between pages, where the document is to be folded into a large section and stapled, since the pages at the bottom of the folded stack will need more space between the text than those at the top. Figure 17.1 illustrates various binding methods. These are briefly described in the following paragraphs.

Ring Binding

This method is favoured for small publications, training manuals and technical documentation. It has the advantage of being easy to do in-house, it is relatively cheap, and is suitable for any publication that requires regular updating. Ring binding also enables the publication to lie flat on a surface which makes a document that is required for constant reference easier to use.

Popular sizes of ring binders are A4 and A5. Most technical and computer software documentation requires A5 size. Many organisations have special binders produced with blocking or silk-screen printing, and/or printed inserts encapsulated on the outside to

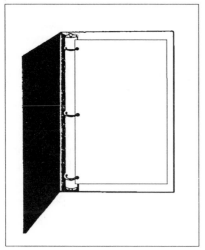

Ring Binding   Stapled

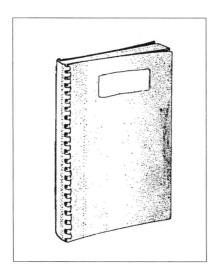

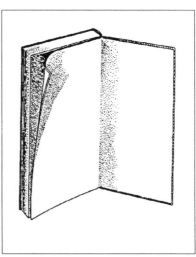

Comb Binding   Case Binding (Hardback)

Figure 17.1   Print Binding Examples

identify the product or the contents of the publication. The number of rings in a ring binder varies. The more rings in the binder, the more secure the paper within it. 'D' shaped rings are also better for holding large documents, since they stack flat against the binder and do not curve around as with an 'O' ring. The capacity of the binder must be sufficient to cope with the size of the publication, otherwise the pages become damaged. The weight of the paper may affect the capacity too.

Mechanical Binding

This can take several forms from comb binding to wiro-binding or plastic gripper. These are all binding methods which can be carried out in-house if the quantities of the publication are not too large. Comb binding and heat-seal binding are popular methods for presenting company reports, quotations, product details, CVs, etc. Both are available from most office suppliers as desktop systems, and heat-sealing is becoming a favourite over comb-binding for high quality presentations. Note, however, that heat-sealed documents do not lie as flat as comb-bound publications, so leave larger margins at the centre of the pages to compensate for this.

Comb binding devices are suitable for documents of varying sizes, and the capacity of combs changes according to the size of the job to be bound. The position of the punched holes at the edge of the paper can also be altered; they can be punched much closer to the edge of the paper and still provide a strong binding, compared to ring binding.

Grippers, like heat-seal bound documents, do not allow publications to lie flat, and have a tendency to spring open if the capacity is stretched to its limit. Therefore, give plenty of room in your centre margin for the document to be opened without having to put a strain on the binding.

Wiro-bound documents are usually assembled using the machinery of a print finisher. It is not a cheap method of binding, but is stronger than comb binding, while having the same advantages of opening flat and requiring narrower margins than other forms of binding. Wiro binding is often used for reference manuals and literature which requires constant use, but may also require the presentation quality which is achieved by this higher-quality binding method.

Perfect Binding

Most paperbacks are perfect bound. This method employs the use of glue to hold folded and gathered sections together with the cover. The back of the folded pages are usually trimmed and roughened to help key the sections to the cover as a complete block, when the adhesive in applied.

The advantage of this method is that it provides a professional look and is a relatively cheap method of binding where large numbers of a publication need to be bound. The disadvantages include a tendency for the sections to become unstuck, particularly if the publication is used regularly, and, therefore this method of binding not suitable for reference documentaion or training manuals.

Sewn Binding

With this method, after the sections of a publication are gathered and folded, a sewing machine inserts threads through the spine of each section and then uses another thread to sew the sections together, to form a single block. This is then glued to the cover like a perfect bound book.

The advantage over unsewn perfect binding is that the pages are more likely to stay together since they have the added strength of the thread. This method is employed in both paper and hardback bound publications.

Case Binding

Case bound books are nearly always hard-back books. The 'end papers' are glued onto the first and last sections, which are glued down to the case. The sections themselves are stitched in the same way as described above, but a linen or paper lining is glued to the spine to help reinforce the joint where the case is applied. Head and tailbands (folded strips of cloth inserted at the top and bottom of the spine beneath the lining) may be used to make the binding look more attractive. The book block can then be left with a flat spine, or may be rounded and backed which gives a firm grip to the sections and helps prevent the middles of sections from dropping forward. Case binding is usually reserved for special quality publishing or where the publication quantity is relatively low.

Appendix

GLOSSARY OF TERMS

The following are some of the terms associated with desktop publishing and typography that you may find useful.

Alignment

This refers to the position of text on a page or within a column. It may be aligned left (ranged to the left and ragged right), centred, aligned right (ranged right and ragged left) or justified (text lined up on both left and right). See also *Quadding*.

Anchor

A specific position on a page may be defined as an anchor point to which, for example, a graphic may be associated. This means that if the layout of the page changes the graphic stays fixed to its specified anchor point.

Ascender

This is the part of a lower case letter that rises above its main body or x-height (see also *x-height*), with such letters as b, h and d. See also *Descender*.

Baseline

Different typefaces vary in size and style and, so that they can be mixed on the same line, are aligned on an imaginary horizontal reference line known as the baseline. See example shown below.

H H H H

Bit-mapping

This relates to the building up of an image using a matrix of dots. Scanners and laser printers use bit-mapping for processing graphics. The quality of the image produced is dependent on the resolution or density of dots in a given area. This is usually expressed as a number of dots per inch, for example 300 dpi.

Bleed

A graphic image may be placed on a page such that it extends beyond the page edge. If the document is reproduced by a commercial printer, the excess paper is cut off when the page is trimmed to size, and the graphic consequently extends to the very edge of the paper.

Bromide

This is the photo-sensitive paper on which the output of a photo-typesetter is developed through a processor, not unlike a film processing system. In fact, the term 'film setting' is still used by some people, and the bromides are referred to as the film output.

Cicero

This is a unit of measurement that is common in Europe. It is equivalent to 4.55 millimetres or 0.178 of an inch and is used for measuring type. See also *Point System*.

Clipboard

This is where text or graphics that have been 'cut' are temporarily stored by DTP systems. See also *Cut and Paste*.

Condensed Type

This is not often available on DTP systems but is found as a facility on some digital phototypesetters. The term itself refers to the relative narrowness of characters in a particular typeface. For a digital typesetter, changing what is known as the 'set width' can invoke the condensing of the characters. For example, a 14-point character can be defined as having a set width of 12 points, which reduces the size of the character's width rather than simply adjusting the space between the characters.

Crop Marks

These are the small lines that indicate the corners of a page when the page is smaller than the paper on which it is printed. They are used as guides for trimming the page to its correct size and may also be referred to as tick or trim marks.

Cut and Paste

This phrase, used often in DTP systems, describes the facility of 'cutting' a piece of text or graphic, therefore removing it from the page, and then 'pasting' it in another place. Before the advent of DTP and WYSIWYG screens this process used to be done manually, literally cutting and then pasting into position with adhesive.

Descender

This is the part of a lower case character that hangs below its main body or x-height (see also *x-height*), with such letters as g, y and p. See also *Ascender*.

Discretionary Hyphen

This is a hyphen, placed in a word at an appropriate point, so that the system hyphenates the word if it does not fit properly at the end of the line. If the word does fit properly or, for example, more text is added which places the word on the following line anyway, the hyphen does not appear. See also *Hyphenation*.

Downloadable Fonts

These are fonts that are bought separately and installed, to in-crease the variety of typefaces that are available on the printer. They may also be referred to as 'soft' fonts.

DTP

This stands for desktop publishing, which is the use of an elec-tronic system, usually based on microcomputer technology, for the purpose of producing high-quality printed matter, which may include text, lines and graphic images.

Em Dash (—)

The size of this dash is the body width of the type size currently being used. It is used as a punctuation mark to break off one phrase from another where they do not flow naturally.

En Dash (–)

An en dash is half the size of an em dash. See *Em Dash.*

Em Space

See *Fixed Spaces.*

En Space

See *Fixed Spaces.*

Expanded Type

This is effectively the opposite to condensed type. For digital type-setters, altering the set width can cause the characters of a particu-lar typeface to be expanded horizontally so as to occupy more width, for example, a 12-point character with a set width of 14 points.

Fixed Spaces

In typography, where certain fixed spaces between characters are required, a system of fixed spacing based on points of space is employed to adjust the space between words or characters that is otherwise variable, depending upon the justification of the text on the line. There are three commonly used spacings:

- em space — generally, space which is equivalent to the value of the point size, so that a 14-point em space will be 14 points wide;

- en space — this is half an em space;

- thin space — this may be either one quarter or one third of an em space.

These spaces are used to make adjustments where additional fixed space is required, for example the first line of most of the paragraphs in this book are indented from the left-hand margin.

Folio

The folio is the page number, usually placed at the top or bottom of a page, which may be aligned right, centred or aligned left according to the page layout. Folio is an old printing term for a page or sheet. See also *Footer* and *Header*.

Footer

This is usually a piece of information placed at the bottom of each page, though it may include a graphic, such as a line or logo, and it is often used to show such things as the page number, name of the publication, etc. It may also be called a trailer or running footer. See also *Header*.

Fount (Font)

A complete set of characters in the same typeface and size,

including letters, punctuation and symbols. For example, 12pt Garamond is a different fount to 12pt Garamond italic, or 12pt Univers, etc.

Frame

A non-printing border which defines the limits of a column of text or graphic image on the page. When displayed on the screen as faint dotted lines, frames are particularly useful when working with multiple-column documents, to see where the limits of text and graphic column boundaries are in relation to one another.

Galley

The word galley is generally only used in phototypesetting, since it refers to a continuous length of typeset material which may be used for proofing or cutting and pasting into position according to the layout requirements. Whereas DTP systems are designed to control the format and layout of the text before output, commercial typesetters would often provide the setting as lengths of text, set at the appropriate width. If this was then required for a manual, for example, the galley would need to be cut to the size of the pages, in order to achieve pagination and the text would then be pasted into its correct position on the pages.

The term galley originates from the 'hot metal' process of type-setting, where a metal tray with raised edges was used to hold about 20 inches of metal type. In this context galley referred to the amount of text set, but the word is more generally used to define the status of a job, ie a job which has reached 'galley stage'. For example, in book publishing it is usual for a book to be set in galleys, then these are proofed back to the author for checking. Once the final setting alterations are made, the galley is turned into paginated or formatted output according to the design requirements of the job.

Graphic

Lines, rectangles, squares or circles created using the drawing tools of a desktop publishing system are graphics. They may also be bit-mapped images, either created using the DTP system or imported from another application or scanner. See also *Bit-mapping.*

Greeking Text

When a page layout is reduced in size on the screen, often to facilitate the viewing of the full page area, the text may be represented as shaded blocks which exactly match the line breaks and position of the text. This may be necessary if the size of the text is too small at the reduced view to read legibly. Text displayed in this way is said to be 'greeked'.

Gutters

This refers to the space between columns in a multiple-column page layout.

Hairline

The thinnest possible rule (line), which is usually 0.25 of a point.

Half tone

A printed illustration usually produced photographically, in which lights and shades of the original are represented by small and large dots, or varying concentrations of dots or lines.

Header

This is usually a piece of information placed at the top of each page, though it may include a graphic, such as a line or logo, and it is often used to show such things as the page number, name of the publication, chapter heading, etc. It may also be called a running header. See also *Footer.*

Hyphenation

This is the process of deciding where to hyphenate the last word on a line. Some systems will do this automatically, based on a hyphenation dictionary, but you may wish to override this and include your own. See also *Discretionary Hyphen.*

Icon

A small graphic image on the screen that represents a function, object or pointer tool. For example, the image of a pencil to represent the tool for drawing.

Indents

Space defined at either end of the line to change the placement of the text. The most common form of indent is for a paragraph denoting the beginning of a block of text. Generally, you should make the indent space proportional to the length of the line, for example:

lines under 24 picas wide   — indent 1 em space
lines between 25—36 picas wide — indent 1½ em spaces
lines 37 picas wide or over   — indent 2 em spaces

Justified Text

Text that is aligned on both the left- and right-hand margins of the document, as used in this book.

Kerning

Kerning is the reduction of space between characters of a typeface in order to improve the appearance when certain pairs of characters appear together. For example, the letter W, when typeset, has a certain amount of optical space beneath the slant of the right and left downstrokes, and this can vary from typeface to typeface. If the letter following it, for example, is set with the normal letter-spacing, it can appear to be displaced too far to the right. By subtracting points of space from between the characters, for example, the following letter effectively overlaps into the set width of the W, making the appropriate optical correction.

Paired kerning is the term used where a composition software system identifies the pairs of characters that require space adjustment and applies kerning automatically, provided that the facility is switched on. Generally, the kerning requirement is more noticeable the larger the size of the typeface.

Leader

These are dots or dashes that fill the blank space left on a line and are usually inserted automatically by the DTP system when specified, for example:

Chapter 1 .... Good Design for DTP Users

Leading

The amount of vertical space, expressed in points, between the baselines of two lines of text (it is pronounced 'ledding').

Letter spacing

This is the term that refers to the amount of space between individual letters, and on most phototypesetters is adjusted by subtracting or adding points of space. This is known as negative or positive letter spacing respectively. Positive letter spacing may be used to put space between the letters of words, rather than have larger gaps between the words themselves which might make them look spread along the line width. Sometimes, positive letter spacing may be used to achieve a particular effect, for example, to space out the characters of a heading.

Generally, positive letter spacing interrupts the legibility of the text, so negative letter spacing is the more commonly used adjustment. This is used to tighten the spacing between letters to improve the appearance of the text, adjust space for *kerning* or to fit copy into a tight space.

Macros

A term used to describe a simple function (perhaps a single or combination of keystrokes) which performs a series of much more complicated tasks, which are usually user-definable.

Mouse

This is a mouse-sized pointing device moved by hand on a desktop surface, which controls the position of a cursor or pointer on the screen in relation to the movements of the mouse itself. It also has up to three buttons on the top which can invoke various functions or selections. A mouse may either mechanically or optically translate its movements into co-ordinates for the screen cursor; optical mice require special surfaces on which to operate.

Page Description Language (PDL)

This is a software facility which is independent of the hardware of desktop publishing systems. It is used to convert a screen image which may include text and graphics, into instructions that can be used to drive an output device like a laser printer. Using such an independent interface allows control over text and graphics, and multiple typestyles and sizes. PostScript is probably one of the best known page description languages, and is generally regarded as the current standard. It has been adopted by a wide range of manufacturers, including IBM and Apple, and offers a path to phototypesetting from PC front ends. PostScript was developed by Adobe. Other PDLs include Xerox Interpress, Imagen Impress and Imagen/HP DDL.

Page Make-up Software

This is software that can produce 'compound documents' which comprise text and graphics together. Using the concept of electronic paste-up, page make-up software can use text files generated on a word processor for pasting into a page layout. Graphics can be imported in a similar way or may be scanned in directly. Page make-up software normally uses a page description language. The distinction of such a package is that text-only software, such as a word processor, has limited output capabilities without a PDL, and provides limited control over layout and typefaces.

Pagination

Pagination is the process of assembling text, graphics, running headers, folios, etc, to produce pages of the required length ready for printing. This can be done by cutting and pasting-up setting and illustrations, etc, by hand, or electronically using a DTP or phototypesetting system.

Pi Characters/Founts

These are special characters or symbols such as ¼, ½, ¾, +, @, <, >, etc. These may be used for mathematical requirements in text, or simply for decorative purposes.

Pica

A measurement equal to one-sixteenth of an inch.

Point System

A point is a unit of measurement generally considered to be equal to one seventy-second of an inch. However, there have been three point systems introduced:

- the American/British system — point is measured as 0.1383 inch, or one twelfth of a pica (pica being 0.166 inch);

- the Didot system — basic unit is the cicero, which is equal to 12 corps (points) or 0.178 inch. The Didot corps measures exactly 0.01483 inch;

- the Mediaan System — point (or corps) measures .01374 inch.

For general purposes, it is useful to remember: 6 picas to one inch, 72 points to one inch and 12 points to one pica. These, however, are not strictly accurate conversions since the point does not directly relate to inches.

Portrait/Landscape Format

Terms referring to the orientation of a page when printed. Portrait meaning the page is printed so that the longest sides are vertical (like the pages of this book), landscape is such that the sides of the page are the shortest.

Proportional Spacing

Spacing between individual characters so that each character has an amount of horizontal space on the line proportional to the width of the character itself. For example, the letter i will need much less space than the letter m.

Quadding

A term relating to the placement of text. The word originates from 'quadrat', which was a metal cube used for filling blank spaces in hand typesetting. Quads, therefore, are used to specify where the remaining space on a line is to be positioned.

This is quad left

                                                        This is quad right
                          This is quad centre

Roman

Ordinary letters, as distinct from italic, bold, etc.

Rules

A term used in printing and design to refer to horizontal or vertical lines, for example as used in forms.

Serif/Sans Serif

Serifs are the short lines drawn at right angles to, or obliquely across, the ends of stems and arms of letters. The term is also used to describe typefaces that have this feature (eg *Times*). Sans serif is a typeface without serifs (eg Helvetica).

Set Width

The set width of a character relates to its point size, so a 9pt character has a set width of 9 points. Some typefaces, however, are designed with a narrower set width, eg 9pt with 8.5-point set width.

Small Caps

These are capital letters designed to match the x-height of a typeface, though many founts these days do not have small caps, so they are created by reducing the point size to 80% of its original size. They are used for abbreviations of awards, titles, etc, following a name, or where whole words in text are set in all caps.

CAPS and SMALL CAPS

Soft Fonts

See *Downloadable Fonts.*

Style Sheet

All the styles that describe the design of a publication's layout and typefaces stored as a group, either in a file format or associated with a macro *(see Macro).*

Superior/Inferior Characters

These terms relate to characters usually set in a smaller size to the text typeface, and positioned above (superior) or below (inferior) the baseline. They are often referred to in DTP systems as superscripts and subscripts respectively.

$$A^2 \quad B_4$$

Tags

Labels given to paragraphs and other elements of a document

which relate to a particular set of formatting instructions. For example, a paragraph tag may relate to the instructions that define the typeface, size, line length, spacing and other attributes.

Template

Actually a style sheet, but often used as a model layout for similar publications. Some desktop publishing software packages provide a number of templates suitable for particular applications, such as, reports, magazines, pricelists, etc (*see Style Sheet*).

Typesize

Typesizes are described by the basic unit of measurement, the point. Points are used to define the length of a metal block or chunk of type. The length of the metal block's top surface relates to the point or typesize, though the character cast onto the surface, will be smaller than the overall size of the metal. Traditionally, then, the point size of a typeface refers to the dimension of the metal block, not the height of the image. This is to allow room for the ascenders and descenders. Thus the typesize relates to the distance between the top of the ascender and the bottom of the descender of the typeface.

Typography

The design of printed matter. A typographer is one who is responsible for the character and appearance of printed matter.

Weight

The weight of a typeface varies according to its design. The thickness of a line will determine how light or dark its image will appear after printing. There are standard terms for the various weights of a typeface and these are referred to as extra-light, light, semi-light, regular, medium, semi-bold, bold, extra-bold and ultra-bold. However, these variations are not standard for all typefaces. For example, 'medium' weight of one typeface may be the same weight as 'bold' in another.

Widows and Orphans

An orphan is the term used to describe the first line of a paragraph at the foot of a page when it is separated from the remainder which may be on the following page. A widow is the term used to describe the last line of a paragraph which appears at the top of a page, separated from the remainder which may be on the previous page.

Word Spacing

In phototypesetting the space between words is variable (unlike a typewriter where the spacing is fixed), which enables lines of text to be justified. It also allows for the optimum number of words to be set on the specified line length.

WYSIWIG

(W)hat (Y)ou (S)ee (I)s (W)hat (Y)ou (G)et. This term is used to describe a feature of word processors or desktop publishing software systems that can represent on the screen display, what the actual output document will look like. The degree of accuracy in this respect, however, varies greatly from system to system.

x-height

This is the height of the letter x and is used to describe the height of the body of lower case characters in a particular typeface. A change in x-height can affect the apparent size of typefaces that are actually the same size.

Zooming

The act of enlarging or reducing the view of a page layout. Enlarging the view of a portion of the document helps when working on detailed items, reducing the view allows the whole page or a pair of pages to be seen in full on the screen to check the overall appearance of the layout.

Index